《论语》移译

The Analects of Confucius in Translation

王金安 译著

东北大学出版社

·沈阳·

前　言

　　21 世纪以来，随着我国的发展和崛起，中华传统文化日益受到世人高度关注，孔子学院似雨后春笋般在世界各国纷纷出现。《论语》这部承载着中国厚重文化积淀的传统经典，在当下正受到海内外学者的空前关注，学习《论语》的人也与日俱增。在此大背景下，译介中国典籍精华，有助于世界其他民族更好地重新认识《论语》，认识中国，也认识自身，从而促进世界和谐发展。

　　《论语》是一部以记录我国春秋时期思想家、教育家孔丘及其弟子言行为主的书，比较集中系统地反映了孔子的儒家核心思想。该书是我国第一本语录文体，内容涵盖哲学、政治、教育、礼仪、文学以及立身处世等方面的内容，被奉为中国人生教科书，也是中国文化的一种象征。全书共二十篇，每篇有若干章，总共 512 章。每篇的小标题系后人取自该篇第一章第一句前两个字或三个字编写而成的。每篇各小节前都冠以序号，条例非常清晰。

　　余长期致力于《论语》译事，常反复研读文本，熟悉其思想背景，会心于原作精神，在汲取前人经验与智慧的基础上，将《论语》全书移译成汉英两种文字，推出一个文白汉英双译本。鉴于此，本书编写格式采用三维一体的形式，即原文、汉译、英译三部分。汉语白话译文力求理解孔子的原意，尽可能完整准确地传达原文意思，复述出原作内容，引导读者深度了解原文神髓，窥视儒学的真精神；英语译文以"存真"为要旨，紧扣《论语》原文，透过字面把字里行间的意蕴曲达地译出，求达原文之语意，保存原作之丰姿，实现达意传神之目的。

　　《论语》原文经过二度翻译，实现了从"语内翻译"到"语际翻译"的转换。本书译文语言体现了原文口语风格，句子结构短小，文字简约，可读性强；译文篇章结构衔接自然，语篇意义前后连贯。此外，为了让读者理解与欣赏，译者对译文中的字、句、章进行了反复推敲琢磨，每译完一章，往往再三咀嚼，看译文有无晦涩暧昧之处，语调读之是否调和顺口，尽量以明白晓畅之字句传达原文之意趣，通过字、句、章的巧妙配合保存原作之神韵，再现原作之风格。本书为"中央高校基本业务费专项资金资助（2015JDZD15）"研究成果。

时代在变迁，社会在进步，《论语》的翻译就这样不断地为时代推进。然而，《论语》话语圆融阔大，语言生动活泼，含蓄隽永，寓意深远，时空跨越两千五百多年，即使后人意会得完整，也难说得准确精当。书中译文若有不妥之处，还望各位读者及同人批评指正。

江南大学外国语学院　王金安

2016 年 5 月 12 日

目　录

学而篇第一

1.1

【原　文】

子曰："学而时习之，不亦说乎？有朋自远方来，不亦乐乎？人不知而不愠，不亦君子乎？"

【汉　译】

孔子说："学习知识之后，在适当的时候温习它，这不是令人愉快的事吗？有好朋友从远处而来，不也是令人高兴吗？别人不理解我，我也不怨恨在心，这不也是一位很有修养的人吗？"

【英　译】

The Master said, "Isn't it a feeling of satisfaction , having learned something, and then practicing it in due course? Isn't it a pleasure to have friends coming from a distance? Is it befitting a gentleman not to resent when others can't appreciate your abilities?"

1.2

【原　文】

有子曰："其为人也孝弟，而好犯上者，鲜矣；不好犯上，而好作乱者，未之有也。君子务本，本立而道生。孝悌也者，其为仁之本与！"

【汉　译】

有子说："一个孝顺父母、尊敬兄长的人，而喜欢冒犯长辈和上司的情况是很少的；不喜欢犯上，却喜欢作乱的情况是从来没有过的。君子专心于根本的工作，只要基础的东西建立了，道也就由此产生了。孝顺父母、尊敬兄长这些'孝悌'准则，应是'仁'的根本吧！"

【英 译】

You Zi said, "It is seldom for a man who is good as a son and obedient as a young man to have the inclination to transgress against his superiors; it is unheard of one person who has no such inclination to be inclined to start a rebellion. The gentleman should devote his efforts to the roots. Once the roots are formed, the Way will grow. Showing devotion to his parents and obedience to his brothers is the root for a person to conduct himself."

1.3

【原 文】

子曰："巧言令色，鲜矣仁。"

【汉 译】

孔子说："满口花言巧语，满脸伪善讨好别人的样子，这样的人有很少的'仁德'。"

【英 译】

The Master said, "It is scarcely benevolent for a man with cunning words and an ingratiating countenance."

1.4

【原 文】

曾子曰："吾日三省吾身——为人谋而不忠乎？与朋友交而不信乎？传不习乎？"

【汉 译】

曾子说："我每天多次反省自己——替别人办事尽心竭力了吗？同朋友交往以诚相待了吗？老师传授的知识用心温习了吗？"

【英　译】

Zeng Zi said, "Every day I examine myself several times. Have I done my best when doing things for others? Am I trustworthy while associating with friends? Have I reviewed and practised what my teachers taught me?"

1.5

【原　文】

子曰："道千乘之国，敬事而信，节用而爱人，使民以时。"

【汉　译】

孔子说："治理一个实力雄厚的诸侯国家，应该谨慎办事，恪守信用，节约开支，爱惜人才，叫老百姓服劳役要不误农时，在农闲进行。"

【英　译】

The Master said, "While administering a country of a thousand military chariots, you should approach your duties with reverence and keep trustworthy as for what you say, also keep your promises, cut down expenses and cherish talented people, and employ the labour of the farmers in the appropriate seasons."

1.6

【原　文】

子曰："弟子，入则孝，出则悌，谨而信，泛爱众，而亲仁。行有余力，则以学文。"

【汉　译】

孔子说："年轻人在父母身边就应孝顺父母，出门在外就要敬爱兄长，做事要谨慎，说话要诚实，要广泛去爱众人，亲近那些有仁德的人。这样做好了以后还有精力的话，就去学习文献知识。"

【英 译】

The Master said, "A young man should show filial devotion and obedience to his parents at home; while out of home, he should obey his brothers and teachers. He should also be cautious about words and deeds, keep honest and reliable and taciturn, show universal love to the broad masses and keep close to the noble-minded people. After all these activities, if he has any energy to spare, let him learn more knowledge."

1.7

【原 文】

子夏曰："贤贤易色；事父母，能竭其力；事君，能致其身；与朋友交，言而有信。虽曰未学，吾必谓之学矣。"

【汉 译】

子夏说："尊重贤者，不重女色；侍奉父母，能够竭尽全力；侍奉君主，能够不惜献出自己的性命；结交朋友，说话诚实，恪守信用。这样的人，即使自谦说自己没有读过什么诗书，我说他一定是读过诗书的。"

【英 译】

Zi Xia said, "If a person shows deference to men of excellence but not to feminine charms, does his best to show filial devotion to his parents, serves his lord without any sacrifice, maintains honest and reliable with friends, I should firmly say that he has once learned the historical documents even if he denies."

1.8

【原 文】

子曰："君子不重，则不威；学则不固。主忠信，无友不如己者。过，则勿惮改。"

【汉　译】

　　孔子说："君子若不稳重，也就没有威严；所学的知识也不牢固。应当把忠信放在首要位置。不要跟与自己不同道的人交朋友。犯了过错，不要怕改正。"

【英　译】

　　The Master said, "A gentleman cannot be a man of high prestige if lacking gravity; what he learns is likely to be flexible. You should do your best for others and be trustworthy as for your words. Do not make friends with those who do not have the same ideals as you. If making a mistake, do not be afraid of correcting it."

1.9

【原　文】

　　曾子曰："慎终，追远，民德归厚矣。"

【汉　译】

　　曾子说："慎重对待父母的丧礼，虔诚祭奠自己的祖先，这样做自然会使老百姓忠厚老实了。"

【英　译】

　　Zeng Zi said, "Cautiously conduct the funeral of your parents and mourn for your ancestors frequently. If so, the virtue of the common people will preserved."

1.10

【原　文】

　　子禽问于子贡曰："夫子至于是邦也，必闻其政，求之与？抑与之与？"子贡曰："夫子温、良、恭、俭、让以得之。夫子之求之也，其诸异乎人之求之与？"

【汉　译】

子禽向子贡问道："咱们老师每到一个国家，必然要过问那个国家的政事。这是他有心求人告诉他的呢，还是别人主动告诉他的呢？"子贡回答道："老师凭温和、善良、恭敬、节俭和谦逊的美德来取得别人的信任和尊敬，使得别人主动把政事告诉给他。先生这种获得别人信任而获知政事的方法，大概与别人获知政事的方法不同吧？"

【英　译】

Zi Qin asked Zi Gong, "When our Master arrives in a state, he always asks about its government affairs. Does he search this information? Or is it given to him?"

Zi Gong said, "The Master gains it through being gentle, kind, respectful, simple, frugal and deferential. His way is perhaps different from that of others."

1.11

【原　文】

子曰："父在，观其志；父没，观其行；三年无改于父之道，可谓孝矣。"

【汉　译】

（在如何评判是否为孝子时）孔子说："父亲在世时，要观察他的志向；父亲去世后，就要看他的行为；如果他能三年奉行父亲生前的行为准则，这样的人就可以称得上孝子。"

【英　译】

The Master said, "You should observe a man's ambition when his father is still alive, and then observe his action when his father is dead. If he doesn't make any changes to his father's ways in three years, he can be considered filial."

1. 12

【原　文】

有子曰："礼之用，和为贵。先王之道，斯为美；小大由之。有所不行，知和而和，不以礼节之，亦不可行也。"

【汉　译】

有子说："礼的应用，贵在处理事情能做到恰到好处。古代圣明君主治理国家，在这一点上做得很好。无论大事小事，他们都能以礼来衡量，以做得恰到好处为目的。但也有行不通的时候，那就是为了求得恰当而一味地恰当，不以礼法加以节制，也是行不通的。"

【英　译】

You Zi said, "Propriety is the most valuable among the things caused by the rites. This is the most beautiful among the ways of the former Kings. If it is followed alike in matters great and small, this will not always work. If aiming always at propriety without regulating it by the rites, one can't work."

1.13

【原　文】

有子曰："信近于义，言可复也。恭近于礼，远耻辱也。因不失其亲，亦可宗也。"

【汉　译】

有子说："与人讲信用符合义，说的话才有可能实现；对别人恭敬符合礼，这样才能避免耻辱。依靠可亲的人，才能靠得住。"

【英　译】

You Zi said, "You should keep trustworthy in accordance with righteousness. As a result, you can put your words into practice. Respectfulness must be closely observant of the rites. Only by this can help you avoid disgrace and insult. You should rely on the relatives as they are reliable."

1. 14

【原　文】

子曰："君子食无求饱，居无求安，敏于事而慎于言，就有道而正焉，可谓好学也已。"

【汉　译】

孔子说："君子吃饭不求饱足，居住不讲究安逸，办事敏捷，说话却很谨慎，接近道德高尚的人来匡正自己，这样可以说是好学了。"

【英　译】

The Master said, "The gentleman doesn't search a full belly and a comfortable home. He is nimble in action but cautious in words. He goes to noble-minded men to have himself put right. If he does like this, such a man can be described as eager to learn."

1.15

【原　文】

子贡曰："贫而无谄，富而无骄，何如？"子曰："可也；未若贫而乐，富而好礼者也。"

子贡曰："《诗》云：'如切如磋，如琢如磨'，其斯之谓与？"子曰："赐也，始可与言《诗》已矣，告诸往而知来者。"

【汉　译】

子贡说："虽然贫穷，却不去巴结奉承别人；虽然很有钱，却不傲慢自大，怎么样？"孔子说："这样也算可以了；但是比不上贫穷却乐于道德的自我完善，富有却又崇尚礼节的。"

子贡说："《诗经》上说：'君子的自我修养就像加工骨器，切了还要磋；像加工玉石，琢了还要磨。'大概讲的是这个意思吧？"孔子说:"赐呀,现在我可以同你谈《诗经》了。告诉了你这一点,你就有所领悟而知道另一点,可以举一反三了。"

【英　译】

Zi Gong said, "Poor without being fawning, rich without being arrogant. How do you think of this saying?" The Master said, "Not so bad, but better still 'poor yet delighting in the way, rich yet observant of the rites'."

Zi Gong said, "The Book of Songs says, 'Like bone cut, like horn polished, like jade carved, like stone ground.' Does it have the same meaning?" The Master said, "I can talk about 'The Book of Songs' with you, as you are able to know the past and foretell the future from what I said."

1. 16

【原　文】

子曰:"不患人之不己知,患不知人也。"

【汉　译】

孔子说:"不要担心别人不了解自己,只怕自己不理解别人。"

【英　译】

The Master said, "Don't be frightened that others don't perceive you. You should be afraid that you don't apprehend others with the mind."

为政篇第二

2.1

【原　文】

子曰："为政以德，譬如北辰，居其所而众星共之。"

【汉　译】

孔子说："国君用道德教化治理国家，他就会像北极星那样，处在自己的位置上，使众多星辰环绕着他。"

【英　译】

The Master said, "On condition that he governs a country by the virtue, a lord can be compared to the Pole Star which is located in its orientation with all stars around him."

2.2

【原　文】

子曰："《诗》三百，一言以蔽之，曰：'思无邪'。"

【汉　译】

孔子说："《诗经》共三百篇，用一句话概括它，就是'内容纯正'。"

【英　译】

The Master said, "Being three hundred in number, *The Book of Songs* can be summed up in one phrase, its thoughts are pure."

2.3

【原　文】

子曰："道之以政，齐之以刑，民免而无耻；道之以德，齐之以礼，有耻且格。"

【汉　译】

孔子说："用行政命令来管理百姓，用刑罚来约束他们，老百姓只会设法避免犯罪，但他们不知道犯罪是可耻的；用道德去教化百姓，用礼教来约束他们，百姓不但有羞耻之心，而且能自己守法。"

【英　译】

The Master said, "If a lord guides his people by edicts and restrains them with punishments, the common people will try to avoid punishment but will lose sense of shame. However, if a lord guides his people by virtue and keeps them in line with the rites, they will bear a sense of shame and try to follow rules."

2.4

【原　文】

子曰："吾十有五而志于学，三十而立，四十而不惑，五十而知天命，六十而耳顺，七十而从心所欲，不踰矩。"

【汉　译】

孔子说："我十五岁时有志于做学问，三十岁时就能自立于社会了，四十岁时已经明了各种事情，不为外界所迷惑；五十岁时知道天命是什么，六十岁时所听到的都能明辨是非，七十岁时，我就可以随心所欲而不会超越法度。"

【英　译】

The Master said, "At the age of fifteen I set my heart on learning the knowledge; at thirty I made some achievements; at forty I didn't feel puzzled any longer; at fifty I perceived the Decree of Heaven; at sixty I could distinguish between truth and falsehood as for what I heard; at seventy I could do as I like without overstepping the principle."

2.5

【原　文】

孟懿子问孝。子曰："无违。"

樊迟御，子告之曰："孟孙问孝于我，我对曰，无违。"樊迟曰："何谓也？"子曰："生，事之以礼；死，葬之以礼，祭之以礼。"

【汉　译】

孟懿子问何谓孝。孔子回答说："孝就是不要违背礼。"

后来樊迟给孔子赶车，孔子便告诉他说："孟懿子向我问什么是孝，我答复他说，不要违背礼。"樊迟问："请问这话是什么意思呢？"孔子说："当你父母健在的时候，应按礼侍奉他们；在父母去世后，应按礼安葬他们，按礼祭祀他们。"

【英　译】

Meng Yizi asked about filial respect. The Master said, "It means 'never going against the rites.'"

Afterwards, Fan Chi drove carriage for his master. The Master told him, "Meng Sun asked me about being filial. I told him that filial respect means not going against the rites." Fan Chi said, "What does that mean?" The Master said, "When your parents are alive, you should serve them according to the rites; when they passed away, you should bury them and offer sacrifices to them as stated by the rites."

2.6

【原　文】

孟武伯问孝。子曰："父母唯其疾之忧。"

【汉　译】

孟武伯问孔子怎样才是孝，孔子回答说："对父母，唯恐他们生病。"

【英　译】

Meng Wubo, a disciple asked about showing filial respect. The Master said, "You are naturally anxious for your parents when they are ill."

2.7

【原　文】

子游问孝。子曰："今之孝者，是谓能养。至于犬马，皆能有养；不敬，何以别乎？"

【汉　译】

子游问孔子什么是孝，孔子说："现在所谓的孝，是仅仅能赡养父母就行了。其实，就连狗马也都能得到人的饲养；倘若没有对父母的一片孝心，那赡养父母与饲养狗马有什么区别呢？"

【英　译】

Zi You asked about filial respect. The Master said, "Nowadays filial respect only means to support the parents. Even dogs and horses are provided with food. So, if a man shows no filial respect, where is the difference between supporting his parents and rearing dogs and horses?"

2.8

【原　文】

子夏问孝。子曰："色难。有事，弟子服其劳；有酒食，先生馔，曾是以为孝乎？"

【汉　译】

子夏问孔子孝是什么，孔子说："子女侍奉父母能经常和颜悦色，这可是件难事。遇到有事情，子女去操劳；有好吃好喝，先让父母享用，这样做就可以称得上孝吗？"

【英　译】

Zi Xia asked about filial respect. The Master said, "The most difficult thing is the reverent expression on one's face. If necessary, you can do something for them; when having food and wine available, you let them enjoy it firstly. It could be considered filial respect to your parents?"

2.9

【原　文】

子曰："吾与回言终日，不违，如愚。退而省其私，亦足以发，回也不愚。"

【汉　译】

孔子说："我整天给颜回讲学，他从来不提出不同的看法，像很愚钝。等到他退下以后，我观察他私下同别人谈话，发现他对我讲的内容很能发挥，可见颜回并不愚笨。"

【英　译】

The Master said, "When I taught Yan Hui all day, he never disagreed with me. He seemed to be just like a fool. However, after he left my presence, I examined his private words closely and found he had developed what I'd taught him. As a result, he is not stupid at all."

2.10

【原　文】

子曰："视其所以，观其所由，察其所安。人焉廋哉？人焉廋哉？"

【汉　译】

孔子："要了解一个人，应看他做事情的动机，观察他做事的方法和途径，还要看他做事的心情。那么，这个人还怎么隐藏得住呢？这个人还怎么隐藏得住呢？"

【英　译】

The Master said, "If you want to perceive a person, you should examine the motives of his words and deeds, observe the way he takes and look closely at where he feels at home. If so, how can a man hide his true character? How can a man hide his true character?"

2.11

【原　文】

子曰："温故而知新，可以为师矣。"

【汉　译】

孔子说："在温习旧知识时，能从中悟出新见解，这样就可以做老师了。"

【英　译】

The Master said, "A man is worthy of becoming a teacher, if he obtains the new insight by restudying the old knowledge."

2.12

【原　文】

子曰："君子不器。"

【汉　译】

孔子说："君子不能像器具那样，仅有某种才艺就行了。"

【英　译】

The Master said, "A gentleman should not be like a tool which only has a certain use."

2.13

【原　文】

子贡问君子。子曰："先行其言而后从之。"

【汉　译】

子贡问怎样做才算是一个君子。孔子说："把自己要说的话先实行了，然后再说出来，这样才称得上君子。"

【英　译】

Zi Gong asked about gentleman. The Master said, "If you want to say a few words, you should put them into effect first and then follow the deed."

2.14

【原　文】

子曰："君子周而不比，小人比而不周。"

【汉　译】

孔子说："君子讲团结，而不与人勾结；小人相互勾结、结党营私，而不讲团结。"

【英　译】

The Master said, "The gentleman unites the masses but doesn't enter into cliques. While the small man gangs up for selfish purpose but doesn't unite the masses."

2.15

【原　文】

子曰："学而不思则罔，思而不学则殆。"

【汉　译】

孔子说："只是读书，而不动脑筋思考，就会受蒙蔽；只是冥思苦想，却不认真读书学习，就会疑惑而一无所获。"

【英 译】

　　The Master said, "If one only studies but does not ponder over, one will be bewildered. On the other hand, if one only indulges in idle dreams but does not study, he'll be perplexed without any gains."

2.16

【原 文】

　　子曰："攻乎异端，斯害也已。"

【汉 译】

　　孔子说："批判歪理邪说，祸害可以消灭了。"

【英 译】

　　The Master said, "As long as one refutes heresy, misfortune will be removed for him."

2.17

【原 文】

　　子曰："由！诲女知之乎！知之为知之，不知为不知，是知也。"

【汉 译】

　　孔子说："由呀！我教你的东西明白了吗？知道就说知道，不知道就说不知道，这才是聪明智慧。"

【英 译】

　　The Master said, "You, do you perceive the meaning of what I have taught you? If you know, say yes; if you don't, just say no. That is wisdom."

2.18

【原　文】

　　子张学干禄。子曰："多闻阙疑，慎言其余，则寡尤；多见阙殆，慎行其余，则寡悔。言寡尤，行寡悔，禄在其中矣。"

【汉　译】

　　子张向孔子请教如何求官做。孔子说："多听别人的意见，把有疑惑的问题先放一旁不说，其余有把握的，也要谨慎小心地说出来，这样就可以减少过失；要多看别人在做什么，把你怀疑的地方暂时搁下不做，其余有把握的，也仍要谨慎小心地去做，这样就能减少懊悔。说话的过错少，行为的懊悔少，求官的秘诀就在这里面了。"

【英　译】

　　Zi Zhang wanted to learn the method of seeking the official posts from his master. The Master said, "Listen more and put aside what is doubtful. As for the rest which you feel confident about, you should speak them out with caution. If doing so, you will make fewer mistakes. Use your eyes more widely and leave out what you doubt about. As to the rest which you are sure of, you should still do them cautiously. If doing so, you will have few regrets. You make fewer mistakes in speech; and you have fewer regrets in action; therein lies the official post."

2.19

【原　文】

　　哀公问曰："何为则民服？"孔子对曰："举直错诸枉，则民服；举枉错诸直，则民不服。"

【汉　译】

　　鲁哀公问道："如何做才能让老百姓服从呢？"孔子回答说："提拔任用正直的人，把他们放到邪曲小人的上面，老百姓就服从了；若举用邪曲小人，把他们放置在正直人的上面，老百姓就会不服从。"

【英　译】

Duke Ai asked, "How to convince the common people?" The Master said, "Promote honest people and set them over the shameless ones. This can make the common people heartily convinced. Otherwise they won't."

2.20

【原　文】

季康子问："使民敬忠以劝，如之何？"子曰："临之以庄则敬，孝慈则忠，举善而教不能则劝。"

【汉　译】

季康子问孔子："要赢得老百姓的敬重，使他们尽忠和互相劝勉行善，该怎么办呢？"孔子说："对老百姓态度庄重，他们就会敬重你；你有孝顺仁慈之心，老百姓对你就会有忠心；你任用品德高尚的人，且教育能力差的人，百姓就会勤勉了。"

【英　译】

Ji Kangzi asked, "How to have the common people treat me respectfully and work diligently?" The Master said, "If you treat the common people with dignity, they will regard you with reverence; if you show filial respect to your parents and kindness to others, the common people will treat you loyally; if you choose and appoint the able persons, educate less capable ones, the common people will work diligently."

2.21

【原　文】

或谓孔子曰："子奚不为政？"子曰："《书》云：'孝乎！惟孝，友于兄弟，施于有政。'是亦为政，奚其为为政？"

【汉　译】

有人对孔子说："您为什么不去做官从政呢？"孔子答道："《尚书》上讲：'孝呀！就是孝敬父母，友爱兄弟，能把这种孝道品德应用到政事上去。'那也就是从事政治，为什么只有做官才算从政呢？"

【英　译】

Someone said to the Master, "Why aren't you engaged in government affairs?" The Master said, "*Book of History* says, 'Being filial means to show filial respect to your parents, while being friendly means to show kind friendship to your brothers.' Exert the principle of filialness and friendship upon political affairs is called being engaged in politics. Why can't this action be regarded as being engaged in politics?"

2.22

【原　文】

子曰："人而无信，不知其可也。大车无輗，小车无軏，其何以行之哉？"

【汉　译】

孔子说："人若不讲信用，真不知道他怎么处世。就好像大车没有輗，小车没有軏一样，靠什么行走呢？"

【英　译】

The Master said, "I do not know how a man can be acceptable if he is untrustworthy. How can the cart be expected to move without a big wooden latch in the yoke-bar of a large cart or a small wooden latch in the collar-bar of a small cart?"

2.23

【原　文】

子张问："十世可知也？"子曰："殷因于夏礼，所损益，可知也；周因于殷礼，所损益，可知也。其或继周者，虽百世，可知也。"

【汉　译】

　　子张问孔子："今后十代的礼仪制度可以预知吗？"孔子说："商朝沿袭了夏朝的礼仪制度，废除和增加了哪些内容，现在通过考察可以知道；周朝又沿袭了殷朝的礼仪制度，废除和增加了什么内容，也是可以知道的。以后有继承周朝的朝代，即使一百代以后的情况，也是可以推知的。"

【英　译】

　　Zi Zhang asked, "Can we expect the rites and systems of the next ten dynasties?" The Master said, "As Shang Dynasty was founded on the rites and systems of Xia Dynasty, the additions and deletions could be known; Similarly, Zhou Dynasty was founded on the rites and systems of Shang Dynasty, the additions and deletions could also be expected. There will have the dynasties which inherit Zhou Dynasty and their conditions can certainly be known even in a hundred dynasties."

2.24

【原　文】

　　子曰："非其鬼而祭之，谄也。见义不为，无勇也。"

【汉　译】

　　孔子说："不是自己该祭祀的鬼神，却去祭祀，这是谄媚。眼见该做的事情而不去做，这是怯懦，没有勇气。"

【英　译】

　　The Master said, "If you offer sacrifices to the spirit of an ancestor who is not yours, you will be thought of fawning on them. If you don't give a hand to what should be done, you will be considered timid."

八佾篇第三

3.1

【原　文】

　　孔子谓季氏："八佾舞于庭，是可忍也，孰不可忍也？"

【汉　译】

　　孔子议论到季氏时，说："他在自己庭院中使用了周天子的八佾奏乐舞蹈，这他都忍心做得出来，还有什么他不能忍心去做呢？"

【英　译】

The Master talked about the Ji family, "He asked eight rows of eight dancers each to perform in his courtyard (This sort of dance was a prerogative of the emperor of Zhou Dynasty). If this can be tolerated, what can't be tolerated?"

3.2

【原　文】

　　三家者以《雍》彻。子曰："'相维辟公，天子穆穆'，奚取于三家之堂？"

【汉　译】

　　孟孙氏、叔孙氏、季孙氏三家大夫，在祭祀他们的祖先结束时，用天子的礼节唱着《雍》诗撤去祭品。孔子说："'助祭的是四方的诸侯，主祭的是庄严肃穆的天子'，这两句话怎么能在三家祭祖的庙堂上唱呢？"

【英　译】

The Three Families, i.e. the three noble families of the state of Lu: Meng Sun and Shu Sun and Ji Sun, they performed *the Yong* after offering sacrifices to their ancestors. The Master said, "'In attendance were the lords. In solemn dignity was the Emperor.' How can *Yong* be sung in the temples of the Three Families?"

3.3

【原　文】

子曰："人而不仁，如礼何？人而不仁，如乐何？"

【汉　译】

孔子说："做人没有仁爱之心，他怎么施行礼仪呢？做人没有仁爱之心，他怎么讲究音乐呢？"

【英　译】

The Master said, "If a person lacks benevolence, how can he put the rites into practice? If a person lacks benevolence, how can he do with the music?"

3.4

【原　文】

林放问礼之本。子曰："大哉问！礼，与其奢也，宁俭；丧，与其易也，宁戚。"

【汉　译】

林放向孔子问礼的本质是什么。孔子说："你提的问题意义很大呀！就一般礼仪来说，与其过分奢侈，宁可朴素节俭；就办丧礼而言，与其仪式上大操大办，不如内心真正悲伤。"

【英　译】

Lin Fang asked about the essence of the rites. The Master said,

"What a significant question indeed! As far as the rites are concerned, it is much better to be thrifty than extravagant. As regards the funeral affairs, the real inner sorrow is more valuable than the inclusive rites."

3.5

【原　文】

子曰："夷狄之有君，不如诸夏之亡也。"

【汉　译】

孔子说："地处偏远的落后国家虽然有君主，还不如中原各国没有君主呢。"

【英　译】

The Master said, "The barbarian tribes have their own lords, which are inferior to the states of central China having no lords."

3.6

【原　文】

季氏旅于泰山。子谓冉有曰："女弗能救与？"对曰："不能。"子曰："呜呼！曾谓泰山不如林放乎？"

【汉　译】

季孙氏要去祭泰山。孔子对冉有说："难道你就不能劝阻一下吗？"冉有回答说："不能阻止。"孔子说："哎呀！难道说泰山神还不如林放，竟会接受季氏越礼的祭祀吗？"

【英　译】

The Ji Sun family went to offer sacrifices to Mount Tai. The Master said to Ran You, "Can't you persuade against him?" Replied, "No, I can't." The Master said, "Alas! Could it be said that the deity of Mount Tai is inferior to Lin Fang?"

3.7

【原　文】

子曰："君子无所争，必也射乎！揖让而升，下而饮。其争也君子。"

【汉　译】

孔子说："君子没有什么事情可争。如果要争的话，那必定是射箭比赛吧！这比赛也是先互相作揖致敬，然后登堂，比赛完后走下堂互相敬酒。这才是君子之争呢！"

【英　译】

The Master said, "There is no competition between gentlemen. If they do have one, it must be a competition of archery. In archery, each side makes a bow first to the other and then steps forward. After the competition, each side makes a bow again and then walks out and finally they drink together. That is the competition between gentlemen."

3.8

【原　文】

子夏问曰："'巧笑倩兮，美目盼兮，素以为绚兮。'何谓也？"子曰："绘事后素。"

曰："礼后乎？"子曰："起予者商也！始可与言《诗》已矣。"

【汉　译】

子夏问曰："'漂亮的脸笑得美啊，明亮的眼睛真妩媚啊，洁白的脂粉把她装扮得好看啊。'这几句诗有什么含义呢？"孔子说："绘画先有白底，再画花。"

子夏说："那么，是不是说礼在仁义之后出现的呢？"孔子说："商，你真能启发我啊！现在我可以和你谈论《诗经》了。"

【英　译】

Zi Xia asked, "'What a sweet smiling face! What a pair of beautiful eyes! Be dressed up with plain face powder.' What is the meaning of these verses?" The Master said, "There comes the plain silk first and then the colors."

Zi Xia said, "Does it mean that the practice of the rites likewise come afterwards?" The Master said, "Shang, it is you who can enlighten me. Only with a man like you can I start discussing *The Book of Songs*."

3.9

【原　文】

子曰："夏礼，吾能言之，杞不足征也；殷礼，吾能言之，宋不足征也。文献不足故也。足，则吾能征之矣。"

【汉　译】

孔子说："夏朝的礼，我能说出来，它的后代杞国不足以作证明；殷朝的礼，我能说出来，它的后代宋国不足以作证明。这是杞国和宋国的文献资料与贤人不够的原因。倘若他们数据充足，那我就可以用来作证明了。"

【英　译】

The Master said, "I can elaborate the rites of the Xia dynasty, but the state of Qi doesn't provide sufficient evidence; I can explain the rites of the Yin dynasty, but the state of Song doesn't supply with the sufficient evidence. That's the reason why there are not enough materials and men of virtue. It's because that there are not enough materials. Otherwise, I can prove what I say with evidence."

3.10

【原　文】

子曰："禘自既灌而往者，吾不欲观之矣。"

【汉　译】

孔子说："禘祭的礼仪，从第一次献酒以后，我就不想往下看了。"

【英 译】

The Master said, "I do not want to see that part of the grand Di held by the lords to offer sacrifices to ancestors, which follows the opening libation."

3.11

【原 文】

或问禘之说。子曰："不知也，知其说者之于天下也，其如示诸斯乎！"指其掌。

【汉 译】

有人向孔子问关于禘祭的道理。孔子说："我不知道呀！知道的人治理整个天下，会像把东西摆放在这里一样容易吧！"孔子指着自己的手掌说道。

【英 译】

Someone asked the Master about the principles of the Di sacrifice. The Master said, "I have no idea. As for the persons knowing them, they are to manage the Empire as easily as to put it here." He pointed his palm while saying.

3.12

【原 文】

祭如在，祭神如神在。子曰："吾不与祭，如不祭。"

【汉 译】

孔子祭祀祖先时，就好像祖先真在那里；祭神的时候，便好像神真在那里。孔子说："我若不亲自参加祭祀而让人代祭，那祭了就如同没祭一样。"

【英 译】

Sacrifices are offered to ancestors as if they were really present; Sacrifices are offered to gods as if the gods were really present. The Master said, "If I did not participate in the sacrifices personally, it was as if I had not sacrificed."

3.13

【原 文】

王孙贾问曰："与其媚于奥，宁媚于灶，何谓也？"子曰："不然。获罪于天，无所祷也。"

【汉 译】

王孙贾问道："与其巴结房屋西南角的奥神，不如巴结灶神，这句话是什么意思？"孔子说："不对。要是得罪了上天，祈祷也没用。"

【英 译】

Wang Sunjia said, "Fawning on the god of the south-west corner of the house, it is not as good as fawning on the kitchen god. What does it mean?" The Master said, "No, this saying doesn't make any sense. When you have offended against the heaven, it makes no difference however you pray."

3.14

【原 文】

子曰："周监于二代，郁郁乎文哉！吾从周。"

【汉 译】

孔子说："周朝的礼仪制度是借鉴夏朝和商朝制定的，是多么丰富多彩啊！我赞同周朝的。"

【英　译】

The Master said, "The rites of Zhou dynasty were made on the basis of the two previous dynasties of Xia and Shang. How luxuriant and colorful it is! I'd like to follow Zhou's rites."

3. 15

【原　文】

子入太庙，每事问。或曰："孰谓鄹人之子知礼乎？入太庙，每事问。"子闻之，曰："是礼也。"

【汉　译】

孔子到了周公庙，每件事都要问一下。有人就说："谁说叔梁纥的儿子识礼呢？他进到太庙，什么事都要问一问。"孔子听到了这话，便说："这就是礼呀。"

【英　译】

When entering the temple of the Duke of Zhou, the founder of the state of Lu, the Master asked questions about everything. Someone said, "Who said that the son of the man from Zou i.e. The Master's father knew the rites? When he went inside the temple of the Duke of Zhou, he would ask questions about everything." On hearing of this, the Master said, "This is in itself the correct rite."

3.16

【原　文】

子曰："射不主皮，为力不同科，古之道也。"

【汉　译】

孔子说："射箭比赛，不在于射透箭靶子，因为每个人的力量大小是不一样的，这是自古以来的规矩。"

【英译】

The Master said, "When one shooting an arrow, the key point doesn't lie in piercing the hide, i.e. the bull's eye fixed in the centre of a cloth target, because everyone has the different physical strength. It's always been the way of antiquity."

3. 17

【原　文】

子贡欲去告朔之饩羊。子曰："赐也！尔爱其羊，我爱其礼。"

【汉　译】

子贡想把每月初一祭祖庙的那只活羊省去不用。孔子说："赐呀！你爱惜那只活羊，我却爱惜那种礼。"

【英　译】

Zi Gong proposed that the living sheep not be killed on the ritual performance of offering sacrifices in the temple of the lord's ancestors on the first day of each lunar month. The Master said, "Ci, i.e. Zi Gong, you care for the sheep, but I cherish the rites."

3. 18

【原　文】

子曰："事君尽礼，人以为谄也。"

【汉　译】

孔子说："完全按照礼节侍奉君主，别人却认为他是在谄媚。"

【英　译】

The Master said, "You will be considered as servile by others if you serve your lord by observing every detail of the rites."

3. 19

【原　文】

定公问："君使臣，臣事君，如之何？"孔子对曰："君使臣以礼，臣事君以忠。"

【汉　译】

鲁定公问孔子道："国君使唤臣子，臣子侍奉国君，该怎么去做好呢？"孔子答道："国君应以礼对待臣子，臣子应以忠心侍奉国君。"

【英　译】

Duke Ding （i.e. the lord of the country Lu） asked, "How should a lord treat his courtiers? And how should the courtiers serve their lord?" The Master said, "A lord should treat his courtiers according to the rites while the courtiers should loyally serve their lord."

3. 20

【原　文】

子曰："《关雎》，乐而不淫，哀而不伤。"

【汉　译】

孔子说："《关雎》这首诗，欢乐而不放荡，哀思而不悲伤。"

【英　译】

The Master said, "The poem *Guan Ju* （i.e. the first ode in the Odes）, it is joyful but not restrained; dispirited but not sorrowful."

3. 21

【原　文】

哀公问社于宰我。宰我对曰："夏后氏以松，殷人以柏，周人以栗，曰，使民战栗。"子闻之，曰："成事不说，遂事不谏，既往不咎。"

【汉 译】

鲁哀公问宰我，制作神主应该用哪一种树木。宰我回答说："夏朝人用松树，殷朝人用柏树，周朝人用栗树，意思是让老百姓害怕得发抖。"孔子听后，对宰我说："已经做了的事情，就不要再解释了，已经完成的事就不要再规劝了，已经过去的事情就不要再追究了。"

【英 译】

Duke Ai of Lu state asked Zai Wo about the altar to offer sacrifices to the god of earth. Zai Wo said, "The men of Xia dynasty used the pine, the men of Yin dynasty used the cedar, and the men of Zhou dynasty used the chestnut (li), saying that it made the common people trembling (li)." On hearing his reply, the Master commented, "We shouldn't explain what has already been done, we shouldn't advise against what has already been completed, and we shouldn't condemn what has already gone by."

3.22

【原 文】

子曰："管仲之器小哉！"

或曰："管仲俭乎？"

曰："管氏有三归，官事不摄，焉得俭？"

"然则管仲知礼乎？"

曰："邦君树塞门，管氏亦树塞门。邦君为两君之好，有反坫，管氏亦有反坫。管氏而知礼，孰不知礼？"

【汉 译】

孔子说："管仲的气量真狭小啊！"

有人便问："管仲生活上俭朴吗？"

孔子说："他有储放钱财的府库，他下属官员一人一职而不兼职，这怎么谈得上俭朴呢？"

那人又问："那么，管仲知礼吗？"

孔子说："国君宫殿门前立有照壁，管仲府大门也立有萧墙。国君设宴招待外国君主，在堂上有放置酒杯的土台，管仲待客也设有这样的土台。假若说管仲知礼，还有谁不知礼呢？"

【英　译】

The Master said, "What a narrow-minded man Guan Zhong was!"

Someone asked, "Was he thrifty, then？"

The Master said, "Guan Zhong had three establishments to hide his money. Even his butlers undertook their own jobs. How could he be considered frugal?"

The man asked again, "Did Guan Zhong know the rites?"

The Master said, "The lord erected a screen wall at his gate. So did Guan Zhong. The lord had an earth terrace on which to put the empty wine-cups, so did Guan Zhong. If Guan Zhong knew the rites, who does not know them？"

3.23

【原　文】

子语鲁大师乐，曰："乐其可知也：始作，翕如也；从之，纯如也，皦如也，绎如也，以成。"

【汉　译】

孔子对鲁国的太师谈关于音乐演奏的道理，说道："音乐，那是可以知道的：刚开始，各种乐器合奏，声音丰美；继而音调和谐悦耳，洪亮清晰，连绵不绝，最后完成。"

【英　译】

The Master talked to the great Musician of Lu state about music, saying, "The principles of music playing can be known to us. At the beginning, you play the musical instruments together and the sound of music is nice; then you continue your music playing, the sound is harmonious, and the scales are distinct; the sound is clear and continuous later. Finally, your music playing reaches the conclusion."

3. 24

【原　文】

　　仪封人请见，曰："君子之至于斯也，吾未尝不得见也。"从者见之。出曰："二三子何患于丧乎？天下之无道也久矣，天将以夫子为木铎。"

【汉　译】

　　仪这个地方的边防长官请求见孔子，他说："凡是到这个地方的贤人君子，我从没有见不到的。"孔子的随从学生带他去见孔子。他出来后，对那些学生说："诸位，何必为失掉官位而发愁呢？天下黑暗无道已经很久了，上天将以你们的老师为圣人号令天下。"

【英　译】

　　The border official of Yi wanted to see the Master, saying, "When any gentleman reaches here, I've never failed to see him." Then the Master's disciples presented him. When coming out, he said, "Why are you worrying about having lost the opportunities to become officials? The Empire has not had the right way for a long time. Heaven is about to regard your master as a sage and let him lead the common people."

3. 25

【原　文】

　　子谓《韶》："尽美矣，又尽善也。"谓《武》："尽美矣，未尽善也。"

【汉　译】

　　孔子谈到"韶"乐时，说道："'韶'乐艺术形式美极了，内容也好得很。"在谈到"武"乐时，说道："'武'乐形式也美极了，不过内容不十分完好。"

【英 译】

When talking about the music named *Shao*, i.e. the music of Shun who came to the throne through the abdication of Yao, the Master said, "Its artistic form is perfectly beautiful and its contents are also extremely good." While talking about the music named *Wu*, i.e. the music of King Wu who came to the throne through overthrowing the Yin dynasty by military force, he said, "Its artistic form is extremely beautiful, but its contents are not so excellent."

3.26

【原 文】

子曰："居上不宽，为礼不敬，临丧不哀，吾何以观之哉？"

【汉 译】

孔子说："处于当政地位的人，对下不宽宏大量，行礼时不恭敬严肃，参加葬礼时不悲伤，这种情形我怎么能看下去呢？"

【英 译】

The Master said, "Some officials lack in tolerance when in higher position, in deep respect when executing the rites, and in deep sorrow when at funerals. How can I tolerate their acts?"

里仁篇第四

4.1

【原　文】

子曰："里仁为美。择不处仁，焉得知？"

【汉　译】

孔子说："居住在有仁者的地方是最好的。选择住处，如果你不选在有仁者的地方居住，那你怎么算得上聪明呢？"

【英　译】

The Master said, "One should live in a place where the benevolent people live. That's the best choice for a man. If he does not settle down among the benevolent people, how can the man be considered wise?"

4.2

【原　文】

子曰："不仁者不可以久处约，不可以长处乐。仁者安仁，知者利仁。"

【汉　译】

孔子说："没有仁德的人不可能长期处在穷困中，也不可能长久处在安乐中。有仁德的人安于仁道，聪明的人知道仁会给他带来好处而实行仁德。"

【英　译】

The Master said, "Persons lacking benevolence cannot remain long in poverty, nor live long in easy circumstances. The benevolent man pursues benevolence because he rests content with it. The wise man implements benevolence because he finds it to his advantage."

4.3

【原　文】

子曰："唯仁者能好人，能恶人。"

【汉　译】

孔子说："只有仁德的人才能喜爱人和讨厌人。"

【英　译】

The Master said, "Only the benevolent man is capable of loving or hating other men."

4.4

【原　文】

子曰："苟志于仁矣，无恶也。"

【汉　译】

孔子说："如果立志实行仁德，就不会做坏事了。"

【英　译】

The Master said, "If a man is resolved to implement benevolence, he will never do evil things."

4.5

【原　文】

子曰："富与贵，是人之所欲也；不以其道得之，不处也。贫与贱，是人之所恶也；不以其道得之，不去也。君子去仁，恶乎成名？

君子无终食之间违仁，造次必于是，颠沛必于是。"

【汉　译】

孔子说："财富和名位，这是人人所向往得到的，但如果不以正当的方法得到它，君子是不会接受的；贫困和卑贱，这是人人所厌恶的，但不用正当的方式抛弃它，君子是不会摆脱的。君子如果抛弃了仁德，又怎么称得上君子呢？君子即使一顿饭的工夫也不会背离仁德，在仓促匆忙之时也总是不忘仁德，在生活困顿、颠沛流离之时也一定按仁德行事。"

【英　译】

The Master said, "Wealth and honors are what everyone wants. Nevertheless, if I got them improperly I would not enjoy them. Poverty and humbleness are what everyone detests. Notwithstanding, if they are improperly removed, we'd rather not get rid of them. If a gentleman lacks benevolence, how can he be called a gentleman? The gentleman never forsakes benevolence just in a short period of time of a meal. If he acts hastily and stumbles repeatedly, he can still implement benevolence in his action."

4. 6

【原　文】

子曰："我未见好仁者，恶不仁者。好仁者，无以尚之；恶不仁者，其为仁矣，不使不仁者加乎其身。有能一日用其力于仁矣乎？我未见力不足者。盖有之矣，我未之见也。"

【汉　译】

孔子说："我没见过喜欢仁德的人，也没见过讨厌不仁的人。喜欢仁德的人，那是再好不过了；讨厌不仁的人，他在行仁德时，不让不仁的人影响自己。有谁能用一天的时间把力量用于行仁德吗？我还没见过力量不够的人。也许会有这种人吧，只是我没有见过而已。"

【英　译】

The Master said, "I've never seen a man who upholds benevolence or one who detests non-benevolence. A man who confirms benevolence will not be outdone. While putting benevolence into practice, a man detesting non-benevolence can prevent those lacking benevolence from affecting himself. Can anyone devote all his strength to benevolence in just a single day? I have never met such a man whose strength proves inadequate for the job."

4.7

【原　文】

子曰："人之过也，各于其党。观过，斯知仁矣。"

【汉　译】

孔子说："人们犯的错误各不相同，什么样的人犯什么样的错误。只要看一个人所犯的错误，就可知他属于哪一类人了。"

【英　译】

The Master said, "Different people made different mistakes. Therefore, you may know what kind of the man by observing his mistakes."

4.8

【原　文】

子曰："朝闻道，夕死可矣。"

【汉　译】

孔子说："早晨明晓了真理，即便当晚死去也值得。"

【英　译】

The Master said, "A person has not lived regretfully who learns the truth in the morning and dies in the evening."

4.9

【原　文】

子曰："士志于道，而耻恶衣恶食者，未足与议也。"

【汉　译】

孔子说："立志探求真理的人，却以自己吃得不好和穿得不好为羞耻，这种人不值得跟他进行交谈。"

【英　译】

The Master said, "A gentleman, who is determined to seek the truth, is ashamed of the humble food and the poor clothes. There is no point talking with him."

4. 10

【原　文】

子曰："君子之于天下也，无适也，无莫也，义之与比。"

【汉　译】

孔子说："君子对于天下的事情，没有规定要怎样做，也没有规定不该怎么做，怎样合理就怎么去做。"

【英　译】

The Master said, "As for his dealings with the world, the gentleman is not consistently for anything or against anything. He may do anything on the side of morality."

4. 11

【原　文】

子曰："君子怀德，小人怀土；君子怀刑，小人怀惠。"

【汉　译】

孔子说："君子常想着道德，小人总思念乡土；君子关心法令制度，小人贪图小恩小惠。"

【英　译】

The Master said, "While the gentleman cherishes morality, the small man clings to his native land. While the gentleman respects the legal system, the small man cherishes his favor."

4. 12

【原　文】

子曰："放于利而行，多怨。"

【汉　译】

孔子说："一切按个人利害关系行事，就会招来众多的怨恨。"

【英　译】

The Master said, "If he does everything just for his profit, a man will incur much resentment."

4. 13

【原　文】

子曰："能以礼让为国乎，何有？不能以礼让为国，如礼何？"

【汉　译】

孔子说："能用礼让来治理国家，能有什么困难呢？不用礼让来治理国家，那又怎样能实行礼呢？"

【英　译】

The Master said, "If a state is governed by observing the rites, it will be easy for you. However, if a state is not governed by observing the rites, how can you put the rites into practice?"

4. 14

【原　文】

子曰："不患无位，患所以立。不患莫己知，求为可知也。"

【汉　译】

孔子说："不要担心自己没有职位，应担心没有胜任职位的才干；不要怕没人了解自己，只求使别人知道自己的本领才好。"

【英　译】

The Master said, "Don't worry about a deficiency of official posts. You should worry about the abilities of earning the positions. Don't worry about the lack of appreciation from others. You should seek the abilities of earning appreciation."

4. 15

【原　文】

子曰："参乎！吾道一以贯之。"曾子曰："唯。"子出，门人问曰："何谓也？"曾子曰："夫子之道，忠恕而已矣。"

【汉　译】

孔子说："参呀！我的学说贯穿着一个基本思想。"曾子说："是的。"孔子出去以后，别的学生问曾子道："这是什么意思呢？"曾子说："老师的学说，就是忠和恕啊。"

【英　译】

The Master said, "Shen! A basic idea is introduced throughout my doctrine." Zeng Zi replied in the affirmative. The master left and his disciples asked, "What's the meaning of his words?" Zeng Shen said, "The central idea of our master's doctrine is but loyalty and forgiveness."

4. 16

【原　文】

子曰："君子喻于义，小人喻于利。"

【汉　译】

孔子说："君子明白的是义，小人懂得的是利。"

【英　译】

The Master said, "The gentleman understands the moral principles while the small man knows just the profits."

4. 17

【原　文】

子曰："见贤思齐焉，见不贤而内自省也。"

【汉　译】

孔子说："看见贤人，就想向他看齐；看见不贤的人，就应当从内心反省，看有没有跟他类似的错误。"

【英　译】

The Master said, "When you meet a person who is better than yourself, you should consider how to learn from him. When you meet a person who is not as good as you are, you should have self-examination in your mind."

4. 18

【原　文】

子曰："事父母几谏，见志不从，又敬不违，劳而不怨。"

【汉　译】

孔子说："侍奉父母时，如果见父母有不对的地方，就应当婉转地劝止；倘若发现父母不愿听从，仍然要恭敬地侍奉他们，不要冒犯父母；虽然内心忧虑，但对父母却不怨恨。"

【英　译】

The Master said, "When serving your parents, you should tactfully try to persuade them against doing wrong. If your parents disregard your advice, you should still treat them with much obedience and reverence.

Though you feel v ery distressed, you still work for them without any complaints."

4.19

【原 文】

子曰："父母在，不远游，游必有方。"

【汉 译】

孔子说："父母在世时，不要长时间出远门。若不得已要远行的话，也应有一定的去处。"

【英 译】

The Master said, "While your parents remain alive, you should not leave home and travel far away. If you do travel away from home, you should tell them your definite destination."

4.20

【原 文】

子曰："三年无改于父之道，可谓孝矣。"

【汉 译】

孔子说："父亲过世三年后，如果能依然信守父亲生前的行为准则，这样的人可以说尽到孝道了。"

【英 译】

The Master said, "A man can still believe in and adhere to his father's doctrine in three years after his father's death, and then he can be called a filial son."

4.21

【原 文】

子曰："父母之年，不可不知也。一则以喜，一则以惧。"

【汉　译】

孔子说："父母的年纪，不能不记在心上，一方面为他们的健康长寿而高兴，一方面又为他们的日渐衰老而忧虑。"

【英　译】

The Master said, "A man should firmly keep the age of his father and mother in mind. On the one hand, he is happy for their good health; on the other hand, he is anxious about their senility."

4.22

【原　文】

子曰："古者言之不出，耻躬之不逮也。"

【汉　译】

孔子说："古人说话不轻易开口，他们认为自己做不到是可耻的。"

【英　译】

The Master said, "In ancient times, men were reluctant to say a few words hastily. They considered it shameful if their deeds failed to keep up with their words."

4.23

【原　文】

子曰："以约失之者鲜矣。"

【汉　译】

孔子说："因为约束自己而犯错误的人是很少的。"

【英　译】

The Master said, "A man who restrains himself strictly can not easily make a few mistakes."

4.24

【原　文】

子曰："君子欲讷于言而敏于行。"

【汉　译】

孔子说："君子说话要谨慎，做事要敏捷。"

【英　译】

The Master said, "A gentleman should be prudent in speech and nimble in action."

4.25

【原　文】

子曰："德不孤，必有邻。"

【汉　译】

孔子说："有德的人不会孤单，一定会有人与他为伴。"

【英　译】

The Master said, "A noble-minded man never feels isolated because he is bound to have his companions to get along with who cherish the same ideals."

4.26

【原　文】

子游曰："事君数，斯辱矣；朋友数，斯疏矣。"

【汉　译】

子游说："侍奉君主过于烦琐，就会招致侮辱；对待朋友过于烦琐，反而会被疏远了。"

【英　译】

　　Zi You said, "You serve the lord too trivially, and it will cause much humiliation for you. Similarly, you treat your friends too trivially, and you'll also become alienated from them."

公冶长篇第五

5.1

【原　文】

子谓公冶长："可妻也。虽在缧绁之中，非其罪也。"以其子妻之。

【汉　译】

孔子评论公冶长时说："可以把女儿嫁给他。虽然他曾被关在监狱里，但那不是他的罪过。"于是，就把自己的女儿嫁给了公冶长。

【英　译】

When making comments about Gong Yechang, the Master said, "It is supposed to marry my daughter to him. Though he was in jail, it was not through any offence on his part." Afterwards, the Master married his daughter to Gong Yechang.

5.2

【原　文】

子谓南容："邦有道，不废；邦无道，免于刑戮。"以其兄之子妻之。

【汉　译】

孔子谈及南容时说："国家政治清明时，他不会被废弃不用；国家政治黑暗时，他也可以免遭刑罚。"于是就把自己的侄女嫁给了他。

【英　译】

When mentioning Nan Rong, the Master said, "When the good governance prevailed in the state, he was not abandoned by the government. When the forces of darkness prevailed in the state, he could be exempted from punishment and released." So then the Master married his brother's daughter to Nan Rong.

5.3

【原　文】

子谓子贱："君子哉若人！鲁无君子者，斯焉取斯？"

【汉　译】

孔子谈及子贱时说："子贱这人真是个君子啊！假如鲁国没有君子的话，他是从哪里获得这样好的品德呢？"

【英　译】

When mentioning Zi Jian, the Master said, "What a real gentleman Zi Jian is! If there were no gentlemen in the state Lu, where could he have learnt his good qualities?"

5.4

【原　文】

子贡问曰："赐也何如？"子曰："女，器也。"曰："何器也？"曰："瑚琏也。"

【汉　译】

子贡问孔子道："您觉得我怎么样？"孔子说："你好比一件器物。"子贡问："那是什么器物呢？"孔子回答说："是宗庙里盛黍稷的瑚琏。"

【英　译】

Zi Gong asked the Master, "How do you think of me?" The Master said, "You're like a utensil." Zi Gong asked, "What kind of a utensil?" The Master said, "Hulian, i.e. an ancient vessel to certain food when offering sacrifices."

5.5

【原　文】

或曰："雍也仁而不佞。"子曰："焉用佞？御人以口给，屡憎于人。不知其仁，焉用佞？"

【汉　译】

有人说："冉雍这个人有仁德，但口才不行。"孔子说："为什么人一定要有口才呢？伶牙俐齿地同别人争辩，常常招人讨厌。我不知道雍是否算得上有仁德，不过为什么非得要有口才呢？"

【英　译】

Someone said, "Ran Yong is a benevolent man, but he is not an eloquent speaker." The Master said, "What's the need to be eloquent at arguing? If he speaks fluently without sincerity, a man will usually incur annoyance from others. I wonder whether Yong is considered to be benevolent or not, but what's the need to be fluent use of language?"

5.6

【原　文】

子使漆雕开仕。对曰："吾斯之未能信。"子说。

【汉　译】

孔子叫漆雕开去做官。漆雕开说："我本人对做官还没有信心。"孔子听了很高兴。

【英　译】

The Master told his disciple named Qi Diaokai to seek the official posts. Qi Diaokai said, "I don't have much confidence in searching for the official posts." The Master rejoiced at hearing this.

5.7

【原　文】

　　子曰："道不行，乘桴浮于海。从我者，其由与？"子路闻之喜。子曰："由也好勇过我，无所取材。"

【汉　译】

　　孔子说："我的主张行不通了，我想乘木排到海外去，能跟随我出去的大概只有子路吧！"子路听了这话后很高兴。孔子说："仲由啊！你的勇敢精神大大胜过了我，可惜你没处弄到编木排的材料呀！"

【英　译】

　　The Master said, "If my ideology were not acknowledged here, I would put to sea on a raft. I suppose that only Zi Lu might follow me." After hearing his words, Zi Lu was filled with great joy. And then the Master said, "Zhong You has nothing to outdo me excepting courage. He can't even find a supply of timber for his raft."

5.8

【原　文】

　　孟武伯问："子路仁乎？"子曰："不知也。"又问。子曰："由也，千乘之国，可使治其赋也，不知其仁也。"

　　"求也何如？"子曰："求也，千室之邑，百乘之家，可使为之宰也，不知其仁也。"

　　"赤也何如？"子曰："赤也，束带立于朝，可使与宾客言也，不知其仁也。"

【汉　译】

　　孟武伯问："子路算得上有仁德吗？"孔子说："不知道。"孟武伯又问。孔子于是说："仲由嘛，可以让他在拥有千乘兵车的诸侯大

051

国去负责军事工作。至于说他是否达到了仁德，我还不知道。"

孟武伯又问："冉求怎么样呢？"孔子说："冉求嘛，可以让他在千户规模的县邑做县长，或在一个拥有百辆兵车的封地做总管。至于他是否达到了仁德的标准，我不晓得。"

孟武伯又问："公西华怎么样？"孔子说："赤呵，可以派他穿着礼服，立于朝廷之上接待宾客。至于他是否具备了仁德，我也不知道。"

【英 译】

Meng Wubo asked, "Has Zi Lu reached the standard of benevolence?" The Master said, "I have no idea." Meng Wubo asked it again. The master said, "Zhong You can be in charge of managing the military levies in a state of a thousand chariots. But I don't know whether he has achieved benevolence or not."

"What about Ran Qiu?" The Master said, "Qiu can assume a steward of a town with a thousand households or a noble family with a hundred chariots. But I still don't know whether he is benevolent or not."

"What about Chi?" The Master said, "Gong Xihua can be a foreign minister who wearing his sash at court and conversing with the guests. But I cannot say whether he is benevolent or not."

5.9

【原 文】

子谓子贡曰："女与回也孰愈？"对曰："赐也何敢望回？回也闻一以知十，赐也闻一以知二。"子曰："弗如也；吾与女弗如也。"

【汉 译】

孔子对子贡说："你和颜回相比，谁更强些？"子贡回答说："我怎敢跟颜回相比呢？颜回听到一件事就可以推知出十件事，而我听到一件事只能推知出两件事。"孔子说："你的确不如他。我和你都比不上他呀！"

【英　译】

The Master said to Zi Gong, "Who is much better between you and Yan Hui?" Zi Gong replied, "How dare I compare myself with Yan Hui? When someone tells him one event, he can know ten events. However, when someone tells me one event, I can only know two events." The Master said, "You are really not as good as Yan Hui. Actually, neither of us is so good as he is."

5.10

【原　文】

宰予昼寝。子曰："朽木不可雕也，粪土之墙不可圬也。于予与何诛？"子曰："始吾于人也，听其言而信其行；今吾于人也，听其言而观其行。于予与改是。"

【汉　译】

宰予白天睡觉。孔子说："腐烂的木头没法雕刻，粪土似的墙壁粉刷不得。对于宰予这样的人，我还能责备他什么呢？"孔子又说："当初我看待一个人，听了他的话便相信他的行为；现在看待一个人，听了他的话后，我还要观察他的行为。经过宰予这件事后，我改变了对人的看法。"

【英　译】

Zai Yu once slept in the daytime. The Master said, "A piece of rotten wood cannot be carved, and a wall of dried dung can not be white-washed by trowels. What's the use to condemn him?" The Master said, "At the outset, I trusted a man's deeds after hearing his words. But now I'll continue to observe his deeds after hearing his words. It was because of Zai Yu that changed my way to observe people."

5.11

【原　文】

子曰："吾未见刚者。"或对曰："申枨。"子曰："枨也欲，焉得刚?"

【汉　译】

孔子说:"我尚未见过坚强不屈的人。"有人说:"申枨是这种人。"孔子说:"申枨私欲太重,他怎么能做到坚强不屈呢?"

【英　译】

The Master said, "I have never met a man who is truly resolute and steadfast." Someone said, "How do you think of Shen Cheng?" The Master said, "Cheng is too selfish and full of carnal desires. How can he be firm and steadfast?"

5.12

【原　文】

子贡曰:"我不欲人之加诸我也,吾亦欲无加诸人。"子曰:"赐也,非尔所及也。"

【汉　译】

子贡说:"我不愿别人把事情强加在我身上,我也不愿把事情强加到别人身上。"孔子说:"赐呀,这可不是你所能做到的。"

【英　译】

Zi Gong said, "While I'm reluctant to be imposed by others, I do not want to impose on others either." The Master said, "Ci, that's beyond what you manage to do."

5.13

【原　文】

子贡曰:"夫子之文章,可得而闻也;夫子之言性与天道,不可得而闻也。"

【汉　译】

子贡说:"老师传授的诗书礼乐方面的知识,我们能够听得到;

老师讲的有关人性和天道的学问，我们却没法听得到。"

【英　译】

Zi Gong said, "We can hear about our Master's systematic knowledge of poetry and books and rites and music, but we can not learn the knowledge of human nature and the Way of Heaven."

5.14

【原　文】

子路有闻，未之能行，唯恐有闻。

【汉　译】

子路在听到一个道理但还没能实行的时候，唯恐再听到一个新的道理。

【英　译】

Whenever he hears something that has not been put into practice, Zi Lu is afraid to hear something new.

5. 15

【原　文】

子贡问曰："孔文子何以谓之'文'也？"子曰："敏而好学，不耻下问，是以谓之'文'也。"

【汉　译】

子贡问道："孔文子凭什么被赐予'文'的谥号呢？"孔子回答说："他这个人聪敏好学，不以向地位比他低下的人学习为耻，因此给他的谥号叫'文'。"

【英　译】

Zi Gong asked, "Do you know why a posthumous title 'Wen' was bestowed upon Kong Wenzi?" The Master said, "He was an intelligent and diligent man who did not consider it shameful to learn from others in humble position."

5.16

【原　文】

　　子谓子产有君子之道四焉："其行己也恭，其事上也敬，其养民也惠，其使民也义。"

【汉　译】

　　孔子说子产具有君子的四种道德品行："他自己行为谦逊，侍奉国君恭敬，养护百姓有恩惠，役使百姓有法度。"

【英　译】

　　The Master said that Zi Chan had the four moral conducts of becoming a gentleman. i.e. he was respectful when conducting himself; he treated his lord with reverence; he gave a favor in caring for the common people, and he was just in employing their services.

5.17

【原　文】

　　子曰："晏平仲善与人交，久而敬之。"

【汉　译】

　　孔子说："晏平仲善于和人交朋友，交往越久，别人越尊敬他。"

【英　译】

　　The Master said, "Yan Pingzhong is adept in making friends with others. He is still respectable even after long acquaintance."

5.18

【原　文】

　　子曰："臧文仲居蔡，山节藻棁，何如其知也？"

【汉　译】

孔子说："臧文仲建自己的宗庙，把大龟壳藏在房顶呈拱形、柱子上画着水草图案的家庙里，这个人怎么算聪明呢？"

【英　译】

The Master said, "Zang Wenzhong built his own temple with an arched roof and columns painted with a design of water plants. A big shell of tortoise was hidden in the shrine of the temple. How can this sort of man be considered wise?"

5.19

【原　文】

子张问曰："令尹子文三仕为令尹，无喜色；三已之，无愠色。旧令尹之政，必以告新令尹。何如？"子曰："忠矣。"曰："仁矣乎？"曰："未知。焉得仁？"

"崔子弑齐君，陈文子有马十乘，弃而违之。至于他邦，则曰：'犹吾大夫崔子也。'违之。之一邦，则又曰：'犹吾大夫崔子也。'违之。何如？"子曰："清矣。"曰："仁矣乎？"曰："未知。焉得仁？"

【汉　译】

子张问道："楚国的令尹子文三次做令尹，见不到他有高兴的神色；三次被罢官，也见不到他有怨恨的神色。卸任前，他一定将自己任上原有的政事全告诉新上任的令尹，这个人怎么样呢？"孔子说："算是尽忠职守了。"子张又问："算有仁德吧？"孔子说："不知道，这哪里算得上仁呢？"

子张又问道："崔子杀了齐庄公，陈文子有四十匹马，他舍弃家产不要，离开齐国到了另一个国家。他说：'这里的当权者跟我们的大夫崔子差不多。'于是又离去。到了另一个国家，他又说：'这里的当权者跟我们的崔大夫一个样。'于是又离开了。这个人怎么样呢？"孔子说："算是很清白了。"子张又问："那算得上仁吗？"孔子说："不知道，这怎么算仁呢？"

【英　译】

Zi Zhang asked, "Zi Wen appeared no pleasure when he served as the premier three times in the state of Chu. He appeared any displeasure when he was dismissed from office three times. Besides, before he was rel ieved from his office, he always told his successor what he had done. How do you think of his action?" The Master said, "He can be said to be a loyal man." Zi Zhang asked again, "Can he be considered benevolent?" The Master replied, "I don't know. How can he be said to be a benevolent man?"

Zi Zhang asked again, "When Cui Zi killed the Lord of Qi, Chen Wenzi who owned ten teams of four horses abandoned his family property and ran away from his own state. Whenever arriving in another state, he used to say, 'The officials here are no better than Cui Zi.' He left again. After arriving in another state, he said again, 'The officials here are the same as Cui Zi.' And then he escaped again. What do you think of his action?" The Master said, "He can be said to be really of noble and chaste character." Zi Zhang asked, "Can he be considered benevolent?" The Master said, "I have no idea. How can he be said to be a benevolent man? "

5. 20

【原　文】

季文子三思而后行。子闻之，曰："再，斯可矣。"

【汉　译】

季文子每办一件事都要考虑多次才行动。孔子听说后，说："考虑两次就行了。"

【英　译】

Ji Wenzi always thought it over time and again before taking action. After hearing this, the Master said, "Thinking twice is quite enough."

5.21

【原　文】

子曰："宁武子，邦有道，则知；邦无道，则愚。其知可及也，其愚不可及也。"

【汉　译】

孔子说："宁武子这个人，在国家太平时他就显得聪明；在国家危乱时，他就装傻。他那聪明，别人可以做得到；他的装傻，别人就很难做到了。"

【英　译】

The Master said, "Ning Wuzi became very clever when peace prevailed in the state. Nevertheless, he could pretend to be very stupid when the state was in turmoil. His intelligence could be learned by others, but nobody could reach his stupidity."

5.22

【原　文】

子在陈，曰："归与！归与！吾党之小子狂简，斐然成章，不知所以裁之。"

【汉　译】

孔子在陈国，说："回去吧！回去吧！我故乡的弟子都志向远大，富有文采，真不知道该怎样去指教他们！"

【英　译】

When staying at the state Chen, the Master said, "Go home! Go home! The young men in my hometown are very ambitious, and also have great accomplishments for their writings. I really don't know how to instruct them."

5. 23

【原　文】

子曰："伯夷、叔齐不念旧恶，怨是用希。"

【汉　译】

孔子说："伯夷、叔齐二人不记以往的仇怨，别人对他们的怨恨也就少了。"

【英　译】

The Master said, "Bo Yi and Shu Qi didn't bear resentment in mind, so they rarely incurred hatred of others."

5. 24

【原　文】

子曰："孰谓微生高直？或乞醯焉，乞诸其邻而与之。"

【汉　译】

孔子说："谁说微生高这个人直爽？有人向他讨点醋，他不直说家里没有，却向邻居讨来转给人家。"

【英　译】

The Master said, "Who said Wei Shenggao was a straightforward man? Once someone begged him for some vinegar, he didn't say that he had none at home. However, he asked his neighbor for some and then gave it to him."

5. 25

【原　文】

子曰："巧言、令色、足恭，左丘明耻之，丘亦耻之。匿怨而友其人，左丘明耻之，丘亦耻之。"

【汉　译】

孔子说："满口甜言蜜语，满脸和颜悦色，显得过分卑恭，对此，左丘明认为这可耻，我也认为这可耻。对人心里怀着怨恨，表面上却与人友好，左丘明认为这可耻，我也认为这可耻。"

【英　译】

The Master said, "Uttering flattering words, showing an ingratiating expression, nodding and bowing too humbly, Zuo Qiuming considers these disgraceful. So do I. Being friendly towards others while feeling resentment in mind, this Zuo Qiuming considers shameful. So do I."

5.26

【原　文】

颜渊、季路侍。子曰："盍各言尔志？"子路曰："愿车马衣轻裘与朋友共，敝之而无憾。"颜渊曰："愿无伐善，无施劳。"子路曰："愿闻子之志。"子曰："老者安之，朋友信之，少者怀之。"

【汉　译】

颜渊、子路两人站在孔子身边。孔子说："你们何不说说各自的志向？"子路说："我情愿与朋友共同使用自己的车马衣服，用坏了也不觉得遗憾。"颜渊说："但愿不夸耀自己的长处，也不表白自己的功劳。"子路说："想听听先生您的志向。"孔子说："我愿使老年人享受安乐，使朋友信任我，使年轻人怀念我。"

【英　译】

Yan Yuan and Ji Lu standing at their master's side in attendance, the Master said, "Why do not you each tell me about your ideals?" Zi Lu said, "I'd like to share my carriage, horses and fur coats with my friends. And I won't have any complaints if they are worn out." Yan Yuan said, "I'd like not to talk about my good points, and not to boast of my achievements." Zi Lu said to the master, "I'd like to hear your ideal." The Master said, "I'd like to bring the peace and comfort to the old, to obtain trust in my friends, and to cherish the memory of young."

5.27

【原　文】

子曰：“已矣乎！吾未见能见其过而内自讼者也。”

【汉　译】

孔子说：“算了吧！我没有见过能够发现自己的过错就在内心自我责备的人呀。”

【英　译】

The Master said, "Let it be! I've never met anyone who is able to find his own errors and then reproaches himself in his mind."

5.28

【原　文】

子曰：“十室之邑，必有忠信如丘者焉，不如丘之好学也。”

【汉　译】

孔子说：“就是在十户人家住的地方，也一定会有像我一样讲忠信的人，只是没有像我一样好学罢了。”

【英　译】

The Master said, "In a small village with just ten households, there is bound to be someone like me who takes honesty as his cardinal principle. Only he is not as eager to learn as I am."

雍也篇第六

6.1

【原　文】

子曰："雍也可使南面。"

【汉　译】

孔子说："冉雍这个人，可以让他做一国之君。"

【英　译】

The Master said, "Ran Yong could be given the seat of a lord."

6.2

【原　文】

仲弓问子桑伯子。子曰："可也，简。"仲弓曰："居敬而行简，以临其民，不亦可乎？居简而行简，无乃大简乎？"子曰："雍之言然。"

【汉　译】

仲弓问孔子子桑伯子这个人怎么样。孔子说："这个人还行，他处事不烦琐。"

仲弓说道："若态度严肃而行事简约，以此来治理百姓，岂不好吗？若态度马虎，办事简约，这不是太简单了吗？"孔子说："你说得对。"

【英　译】

Zhong Gong asked the Master about his impression of Zi Sang Bo Zi. The Master said, "He is an acceptable man because of the simplicity of his style." Zhong Gong said, "Isn't it acceptable for him to administer the common people with reverent attitudes and the simple measures? On the other hand, he has the careless attitudes and the simple actions in his administration. Isn't it for him to be too careless?" The Master said, "What you said makes sense."

6.3

【原　文】

　　哀公问："弟子孰为好学?"孔子对曰："有颜回者好学，不迁怒，不贰过。不幸短命死矣。今也则亡，未闻好学者也。"

【汉　译】

　　鲁哀公问孔子说："你的学生中谁最爱学习?"孔子回答说："有个叫颜回的学生好学，他从不把怨气发泄到别人身上，也不再犯同样的错误。可惜他短命死了。现在没有这样的人了，也没再听说有好学的人了。"

【英　译】

　　As being a lord of the state Lu, Duke Ai asked, "Who was the best one to love learning among your disciples?" The Master replied, "There was one disciple named Yan Hui who was eager to learn. He never transferred the anger made by someone to another person. Nor did he make the same mistake again. Unfortunately he passed away at the young age. Now I haven't met anyone the same as his devotion to learning."

6.4

【原　文】

　　子华使于齐，冉子为其母请粟。子曰："与之釜。"请益。曰："与之庾。"冉子与之粟五秉。子曰："赤之适齐也，乘肥马，衣轻裘。吾闻之也：君子周急不继富。"

【汉　译】

　　子华出使去齐国，冉子替子华的母亲向孔子要点米。孔子说：

"给她六斗四升吧。"冉子请求再多给些。孔子说："那就再给她二斗四升吧。"冉子却给了子华的母亲八十石。孔子说："公西华出使齐国，乘坐肥马驾的车，穿着轻暖的皮衣。我听说过：君子只会周济穷人，而不接济那些富人。"

【英　译】

Zi Hua was sent to the state Qi on a diplomatic mission. Ran Zi asked the Master to give some grains to Zi Hua's mother. The Master said, "Give her 100 pounds." Ran Zi asked for more grains. The Master said, "And then add nearly 30 pounds." The Master said, "Gong Xichi went off to the state Qi in a splendid carriage and was wearing light furs. I have heard it said, 'A gentleman only relieves the poor but doesn't add help out the rich.'"

6.5

【原　文】

原思为之宰，与之粟九百，辞。子曰："毋！以与尔邻里乡党乎！"

【汉　译】

原思在孔子家当总管，孔子给他九百斗俸米，他推辞不肯多要。孔子说："不要推辞啦！可给你家乡的乡亲些吧！"

【英　译】

Yuan Si acted as a housekeeper at the Master's family. The Master offered him 900 pounds of grains, but he declined to receive too much. The Master said, "Don't turn it down. You may give some surplus grains to your country folks."

6.6

【原　文】

子谓仲弓，曰："犁牛之子骍且角，虽欲勿用，山川其舍诸？"

【汉　译】

孔子讲到仲弓时，说："一头耕牛产下的小牛犊周身赤色，两只角长得也端正，人们虽不想用它来祭祀，山川之神难道会舍弃它吗？"

【英　译】

When talking about Zhong Gong, the Master said, "A farm cattle breeds a calf with red fur coat and regular horns. Even if it was not used for sacrificing, the spirits of mountain and river cannot abandon this calf, can they?"

6.7

【原　文】

子曰："回也，其心三月不违仁，其余则日月至焉而已矣。"

【汉　译】

孔子说："颜回呀，其心能长时间不背离仁德，其余弟子则仅能在短时间做到仁罢了。"

【英　译】

The Master said, "Yan Hui does not deviate from benevolence in his mind for a long time. However, the other disciples attain benevolence only for a short period."

6.8

【原　文】

季康子问："仲由可使从政也与？"

子曰："由也果，于从政乎何有？"

曰："赐也可使从政也与？"

曰："赐也达，于从政乎何有？"

曰："求也可使从政也与？"

曰："求也艺，于从政乎何有？"

【汉　译】

　　季康子问孔子："仲由此人，可以让他治理政事吗？"

　　孔子说："仲由办事果断，让他治理政事有什么困难呢？"

　　季康子又问："子贡，可以让他治理政事吗？"

　　孔子说："子贡通达人情事理，让他治理政事有什么困难呢？"

　　季康子又问道："冉求此人，可以让他治理政事吗？"

　　孔子说："冉求多才多艺，让他治理政事会有什么困难呢？"

【英　译】

　　Ji Kangzi asked, "Is Zhong You capable enough to administer the governmental affairs?" The Master said, "You is extremely determined in action. Will there be any difficulties for him to control the governmental affairs?" Ji Kangzi asked, "Is Zi Gong capable enough to administer the governmental affairs?" The Master said, "Zi Gong is a worldly-wise man. Will there be any difficulties for him to control the governmental affairs?" Ji Kangzi asked, "Is Ran Qiu capable enough to administer the governmental affairs?" The Master said, "Ran Qiu is a versatile man. Will there be any difficulties for him to control the governmental affairs?"

6.9

【原　文】

　　季氏使闵子骞为费宰。闵子骞曰："善为我辞焉！如有复我者，则吾必在汶上矣。"

【汉　译】

　　季氏派人请闵子骞到他家费邑去做官。闵子骞对来人说："请好好替我推辞吧！如果再来召我的话，那我肯定逃到汶水北边去了。"

【英　译】

　　The Ji family sent one man to ask Min Zi-qian to act as the steward of his hometown Fei. Min Zi-qian said, "Please turn it down for me. If someone comes back again for me, I'll run away to the other side of Wen River."

6. 10

【原　文】

　　伯牛有疾，子问之，自牖执其手，曰："亡之，命矣夫！斯人也而有斯疾也！斯人也而有斯疾也！"

【汉　译】

　　伯牛有病了，孔子前去探视他，从窗户里握住他的手，说："这人难活了，真是天意啊！这人竟会得这样的病！这人竟会得这样的病！"

【英　译】

　　Bo Niu was ill. The Master visited him and held his hand through the window and said, "This man will lose his life. It is his destiny to die. Why should such a man be stricken with such an illness? Why should such a man be stricken with such an illness?"

6. 11

【原　文】

　　子曰："贤哉，回也！一箪食，一瓢饮，在陋巷，人不堪其忧，回也不改其乐。贤哉，回也！"

【汉　译】

　　孔子说："颜回多么贤德啊！一竹筒饭，一瓢水，住在穷陋的小巷子里，别人都受不了那种苦楚，颜回却不改变其自有的快乐。颜回多么贤德呀！"

【英　译】

　　The Master said, "What a noble-minded man he is! With only a bamboo tube of rice and a ladleful of water, Yan Hui dwells in a faded and worn lane. Most people cannot tolerate this miserable life. But Yan Hui has never changed his optimistic qualities. How virtuous Yan Hui is!"

6. 12

【原　文】

冉求曰："非不说子之道，力不足也。"子曰："力不足者，中道而废。今女画。"

【汉　译】

冉求说："不是我不喜欢您的学说，而是我能力不够。"孔子说："如果能力不够的话，走到半路就走不动了。现在你还没开始，就自己划定界限，停止前进了！"

【英　译】

Ran Qiu said, "It's not that I dislike your doctrine but I don't have great ability." The Master said, "A man lack of a tremendous capacity will stop halfway. You have not started to go, but you're not willing to march forward."

6. 13

【原　文】

子谓子夏曰："女为君子儒！无为小人儒！"

【汉　译】

孔子对子夏说："你应该做君子型的读书人，不要做小人式的读书人。"

【英　译】

The Master said to Zi Xia, "You ought to become a scholar of gentleman but not a scholar of mean man."

6.14

【原　文】

子游为武城宰。子曰："女得人焉耳乎？"曰："有澹台灭明者，行不由径，非公事，未尝至于偃之室也。"

【汉　译】

子游做了武城邑地方长官，孔子说："你在那里求得人才了吗？"子游说："有个叫澹台灭明的人，他处事行正道，没有公事从来不到我屋里来。"

【英　译】

Zi You was the steward of Wu Cheng City. The Master asked, "Have you discovered any talents？" Zi You replied, "I know a man named Tan-tai Mie-ming who never goes astray. And he will never come to my office except for official business."

6.15

【原　文】

子曰："孟之反不伐，奔而殿，将入门，策其马，曰：'非敢后也，马不进也。'"

【汉　译】

孔子说："孟之反不自我夸耀，打仗撤退时留在最后做掩护，快进城门时，他却策马经过欢迎的人群，自谦道：'不是我敢于殿后，是马跑得不快呀。'"

【英　译】

The Master said, "Meng Zhi fan has never been boastful. When the whole army was in retreat, he brought up the rear. But on entering the city gate, he whipped his horse and passed through the greeting crowd, saying, 'It's not that I dare to bring up in the rear but that my horse does not run so fast.'"

6. 16

【原　文】

子曰：“不有祝鮀之佞，而有宋朝之美，难乎免于今之世矣！”

【汉　译】

孔子说：“人若没有祝鮀那样的口才，而仅有宋朝般的美貌，那么在当今世上就难免要受害了。”

【英　译】

The Master said, "A man will never avoid great disasters in the world provided that he isn't as eloquent as Zhu Tuo but he has only got a graceful looks like Song Chao who was the most handsome man in the state Song at Spring and Autumn Warring Period of ancient China."

6.17

【原　文】

子曰：“谁能出不由户？何莫由斯道也？”

【汉　译】

孔子说：“有谁能不从门户外出呢？为什么没有人行走我这条路呢？”

【英　译】

The Master said, "Who can go out of his house without passing through the door? Why does nobody follow my Way?"

6.18

【原　文】

子曰：“质胜文则野，文胜质则史。文质彬彬，然后君子。”

【汉　译】

孔子说：“质朴多于文采，就会显得粗野；文采多于质朴，就会显得虚浮。文采和质朴配合适当，这才是个君子。"

【英 译】

The Master said, "If his sincerity and simplicity outdo his literary grace, a man will say the rude words and behave roughly. On the contrary, if his literary grace outdoes his sincerity and simplicity, a man will have some superficial qualities. Only by means of proper combination of the two qualities can he become a gentleman."

6.19

【原 文】

子曰："人之生也直，罔之生也幸而免。"

【汉 译】

孔子说："人因为正直才能在世上生存，不正直的人也能生存，那是他侥幸地躲过了灾难罢了。"

【英 译】

The Master said, "Because he is upright, a man can live in the world. However, a dishonest man will also be able to live in the world as he can avoid disasters fortunately."

6.20

【原 文】

子曰："知之者不如好之者，好之者不如乐之者。"

【汉 译】

孔子说："（但凡一切学问和事业）知道它的人，不如喜好它的人；喜爱它的人，又不如以此为快乐的人。"

【英 译】

The Master said, "As regards systematic learning and undertakings, just knowing them is not as good as loving them, and loving them is not as good as taking pleasure from them."

6.21

【原　文】

子曰："中人以上，可以语上也；中人以下，不可以语上也。"

【汉　译】

孔子说："中等以上天赋的人，可以给他讲高深的学问；中等以下天赋的人，不可以告诉他高深的学问。"

【英　译】

The Master said, "As for a man above average gift, you can tell him profound learning; as for a man below average gift, you cannot tell him profound learning."

6.22

【原　文】

樊迟问知，子曰："务民之义，敬鬼神而远之，可谓知矣。"问仁，曰："仁者先难而后获，可谓仁矣。"

【汉　译】

樊迟问怎样做才算聪明，孔子说："做事要顺乎民意，至于鬼神则敬而远之，这样才算聪明。"

樊迟又问怎样做才算有仁德，孔子说："有仁德的人对难事抢在别人前面做，有奖赏、收获则退居人后，这样可以说是有仁德了。"

【英　译】

Fan Chi asked about connotation of wisdom. The Master said, "You should work for whatever the common people desire. With regard to the gods and spirits of the dead, you should treat them with reverence and keep your distance from them. And then it can be called wisdom."

Fan Chi asked about the essence of benevolence. The Master said, "The benevolent man should deal with the difficulties before others and enjoy the good things afterwards. And then that can be called benevolence."

6.23

【原　文】

子曰："知者乐水，仁者乐山。知者动，仁者静。知者乐，仁者寿。"

【汉　译】

孔子说："智者喜好水，仁者喜好山。智者喜好常动，仁者喜好恬静。智者内心快乐，仁者健康长寿。"

【英　译】

The Master said, "The wise enjoy water, and the benevolent enjoy mountains. The wise love to be active, and the benevolent love to be calm. The wise are cheerful, and the benevolent are of longevity."

6.24

【原　文】

子曰："齐一变，至于鲁；鲁一变，至于道。"

【汉　译】

孔子说："齐国一变革，可以达到鲁国的样子；鲁国一变革，就可以达到先王之道了。"

【英　译】

The Master said, "Through reformation, the social system of the state Qi can attain the level of the state Lu. And then the social system of the state Lu can reach the right track by means of reformation."

6. 25

【原　文】

子曰：“觚不觚，觚哉！觚哉！”

【汉　译】

孔子说：“觚不像个觚，这还是觚呀！这还是觚呀！”

【英　译】

The Master said, "A Gu does not look like a real drinking vessel. Can it be called a drinking vessel?   Can it be called a drinking vessel?"

Gu: a drinking vessel with a regulation capacity.

6. 26

【原　文】

宰我问曰：“仁者，虽告之曰：‘井有仁焉。’其从之也？”子曰：“何为其然也？君子可逝也，不可陷也；可欺也，不可罔也。”

【汉　译】

宰我问道：“对于仁德之人，有人告诉他说：‘井里掉下去一位仁人。’他会跟着跳下去吗？”孔子说：“为什么要这样做呢？君子可以去井边救人，但不能也陷入井里；君子可以被骗，但不能受别人愚弄。”

【英　译】

Zai Wo asked, "A benevolent man is told that 'a benevolent man has fallen into a well.' Would the benevolent jump into the well in search of him?" The Master said, "Why should he do it just like this? A gentleman can go to the well to save the man, but he should not be lured into the well. A gentleman may be deceived, but he should not be fooled by others."

6.27

【原 文】

子曰："君子博学于文，约之以礼，亦可以弗畔矣夫！"

【汉 译】

孔子说："君子广泛地学习文献知识，并用礼来约束自己，这样就不至于离经叛道了。"

【英 译】

The Master said, "Provided he studies the historical documents exte nsively and is restrained by the rites, a gentleman can avoid being out of the right way."

6.28

【原 文】

子见南子，子路不说。夫子矢之曰："予所否者，天厌之！天厌之！"

【汉 译】

孔子去见了南子，子路不高兴。孔子发誓说："若我的行为不合乎礼的话，天会厌弃我！天会厌弃我！"

【英 译】

The Master went to see Nan Zi, i.e. the notorious wife of Duke Wei Ling. Zi Lu was annoyed. The Master promised solemnly, "If I do something against the rites, may Heaven curse me! May Heaven curse me!"

6.29

【原 文】

子曰："中庸之为德也，其至矣乎！民鲜久矣。"

【汉　译】

孔子说："作为一种道德，中庸可算是最高境界了吧！可人们缺少此德已经很久了。"

【英　译】

The Master said, "The Mean can be considered the highest degree as a moral virtue. But the common people have been in want of this virtue for a long time."

6.30

【原　文】

子贡曰："如有博施于民而能济众，何如？可谓仁乎？"子曰："何事于仁！必也圣乎！尧舜其犹病诸！夫仁者，己欲立而立人，己欲达而达人。能近取譬，可谓仁之方也已。"

【汉　译】

子贡说："假使有人给百姓广施恩惠，救济众生，这人怎么样呢？能称得上是仁者吗？"孔子说："何止是仁人？必定是个圣人啊！就连尧舜恐怕也难以做到呀！仁德之人，自己想立足于社会，也帮助别人立足，自己做事想通达，也帮助别人通达，能做到推己及人，这可以说是为仁的方法。"

【英　译】

Zi Gong said, "If there were a man giving extensively to the multitude and extending relief to the common people, how would you think of him? Could he be called a benevolent man?" The Master said, "It is far more than that. He's certain to be a sage! Even archaic emperors named Yao and Shun couldn't attain this stage. As regards a benevolent man, he is bound to help others find home in society if he himself wants to do; he is sure to help others fully developed if he himself wants to do. So long as he thinks himself back into the shoes of others, he is considered to master a way to put humanity into practice."

述而篇第七

7.1

【原　文】

子曰："述而不作，信而好古，窃比于我老彭。"

【汉　译】

孔子说："只传述旧作而不创新，相信且喜好古文化，我私下自比商朝的老彭。"

【英　译】

The Master said, "I only impart and inherit the archaic works but don't make any innovations; I consistently trust and enjoy the ancient culture; I sometimes compare myself with Mr. Peng of Shang Dynasty in private."

7.2

【原　文】

子曰："默而识之，学而不厌，诲人不倦，何有于我哉？"

【汉　译】

孔子说："默默地记住所学的知识，勤奋学习而不满足，教导别人不知疲倦，这对我来说，有什么困难呢？"

【英　译】

The Master said, "Quietly to memorize something learnt in mind, diligently to learn knowledge unsatisfactorily, consistently to teach others tirelessly. With regard to these above-mentioned, are there any difficulties for me?"

7.3

【原　文】

子曰："德之不修，学之不讲，闻义不能徙，不善不能改，是吾忧也。"

【汉　译】

孔子说："对品德不加以修养，对学问不勤于讲习，听到义之所在却不能迁而从之，有缺点自己不能改正，这些都是我所忧虑的啊！"

【英　译】

The Master said, "Not to improve moral character, not to learn knowledge assiduously, not to go over to where justice exists, not to correct one's own mistakes. With regard to these above-mentioned, they are what I worry about."

7.4

【原　文】

子之燕居，申申如也，夭夭如也。

【汉　译】

孔子闲居在家时，看上去很舒畅，一副悠闲自在的样子。

【英　译】

When staying at home, the Master appeared to be in a more relaxed mood.

7.5

【原　文】

子曰："甚矣吾衰也！久矣吾不复梦见周公。"

【汉　译】

孔子说："我衰老得多么厉害呀！我好久没有再梦见周公了。"

【英　译】

The Master said, "How extremely feeble I have been! I haven't dreamed of the Duke of Zhou for a long time."

7.6

【原　文】

子曰："志于道，据于德，依于仁，游于艺。"

【汉　译】

孔子说："志向在'道'，据守在'德'，依据在'仁'，游习于'六艺'之中。"

【英　译】

The Master said, "I commit myself to the Way, base myself on virtue and benevolence, and take my recreation in the six arts."

7.7

【原　文】

子曰："自行束修以上，吾未尝无诲焉。"

【汉　译】

孔子说："凡是带着十条干肉做见面薄礼来求见我的，我从没有不给予教诲的。"

【英　译】

The Master said, "I've never refused to instruct anyone who has given me ten or more pieces of dried meat as gift in lieu of tuition."

7.8

【原　文】

子曰："不愤不启，不悱不发。举一隅不以三隅反，则不复也。"

【汉　译】

孔子说："教导学生时，不到他心里想弄明白而又想不通的时候，我就不去开导他；不到他心里想说而嘴上又不能说清楚的时候，我不去启发他。举出一个角落讲给他听，而他却不能由此推知还有其他三个角落，那我就不再教他了。"

【英　译】

The Master said, "I will not enlighten a student until he is eager to know a problem but has been puzzled about it. Similarly, I will not inform a student until he can't wait to say but can't speak it out. For instance, when I point out one corner of a room for him, the student can't know the other three corners of the room. With regard to such a student, I will not teach him again."

7.9

【原　文】

子食于有丧者之侧，未尝饱也。

【汉　译】

孔子在有丧事的人旁进食，不曾吃饱过。

【英　译】

When eating in the presence of bereaved people, the Master can never stuff himself.

7.10

【原　文】

子于是日哭，则不歌。

【汉　译】

孔子这一天为吊丧而哭泣过，那他就不再唱歌了。

【英　译】

Because he wept for the dead on this day, the Master would no longer sing a song.

7.11

【原　文】

　　子谓颜渊曰：“用之则行，舍之则藏，惟我与尔有是夫！”
　　子路曰：“子行三军，则谁与？”
　　子曰：“暴虎冯河，死而无悔者，吾不与也。必也临事而惧，好谋而成者也。”

【汉　译】

　　孔子对颜渊说：“有能用我的，则实行我的主张；不能用我的，则将它收藏起来。只有我和你能这样了！”
　　子路说：“先生若率领军队指挥作战，会找谁与您共事呢？”
　　孔子说：“徒手与虎搏斗，徒步涉水过河，死了也不后悔的人，我是不与他共事的。和我共事的，一定是临事能谨慎小心，善于谋划而取得成功的人。”

【英　译】

　　The Master said to Yan Yuan, "If I'm employed, I'll be able to put my views into effect. Otherwise, I'll conceal them. I suppose only you and

I can achieve the ends."

Zi Lu asked, "If you command the armed forces, you will choose what sort of men as your assistants."

The Master said, "I will not choose anyone who would try to wrestle with a tiger barehanded or to walk across a river on foot and die without any regrets. I prefer to choose those who can act prudently and win victory strategically."

7.12

【原　文】

子曰："富而可求也，虽执鞭之士，吾亦为之。如不可求，从吾所好。"

【汉　译】

孔子说："富若合于道而可求，就是去做执鞭贱职，我也愿为。倘若不可求得，那还是从我所好吧。"

【英　译】

The Master said, "As long as properties were obtained in conformity to the Way, I would be willing to acquire them even if I acted as a humble official just like a guard holding a whip. If not, I will follow my own inclination."

7.13

【原　文】

子之所慎：齐，战，疾。

【汉　译】

孔子谨慎行事有三样：斋戒，战争，疾病。

【英　译】

The Master acted prudently in three respects including fasting, war and disease.

7.14

【原　文】

子在齐闻《韶》，三月不知肉味，曰："不图为乐之至于斯也。"

【汉　译】

孔子在齐国听到了《韶》乐，有三个月尝不出肉味，于是说："想不到《韶》乐之美到了如此境界。"

【英　译】

After hearing the music named Shao in the state Qi, the Master hadn't sniffed the taste of the meat he ate for three months. He said, "I've never expected that the music named Shao has reached the acme of perfection."

7.15

【原　文】

冉有曰："夫子为卫君乎？"子贡曰："诺，吾将问之。"入，曰："伯夷、叔齐何人也？"曰："古之贤人也。"曰："怨乎？"曰："求仁而得仁，又何怨？"出，曰："夫子不为也。"

【汉　译】

冉有问道："先生会支持卫君吗？"子贡说："嗯，我去问问他。"
子贡进去，问孔子道："伯夷、叔齐人怎么样呢？"孔子说："他们是古代的贤人呀。"子贡又问："他们互让君位而出逃，后来是不是内心又有怨恨后悔呢？"孔子答道："他们求仁得仁，内心已安，又有什么怨恨呢？"子贡出来说："我们先生是不会支持卫君的。"

【英　译】

Ran You said, "Is our master going to support the lord of state Wei?" Zi Gong said, "Well, I am about to ask him." After entering the room of his master, Zi Gong asked, "What do you think of Bo Yi and Shu Qi?" The Master replied, "They are ancient persons of virtue." Zi Gong asked,

"Did they have any complaints about their past actions?" The Master replied, "They sought benevolence and they obtained it. So why should they feel regrettable?" After going out, Zi Gong said, "Our master wouldn't be on his side."

7.16

【原　文】

子曰："饭疏食饮水，曲肱而枕之，乐亦在其中矣。不义而富且贵，于我如浮云。"

【汉　译】

孔子说："吃着粗粮，喝着白水，弯着胳膊当枕头枕，乐趣也就在这里了。用非正当的手段得到的富贵，对我来说就像天上的浮云一样。"

【英　译】

The Master said, "Joy is found in the course of eating the humble bread and drinking the cold water and using my bended arm as a pillow. Wealth and honors attained by immoral means appear just like the floating clouds in the sky."

7.17

【原　文】

子曰："加我数年，五十以学《易》，可以无大过矣。"

【汉　译】

孔子说："再给我几年时间，到五十岁时学习《周易》，就可以没有大的过错了。"

【英　译】

The Master said, "If I were granted a few more years, I would be about to study *Yi*—the ancient book making divinations using Eight Trigrams (superstitions) at the age of fifty, and I shall probably be free from making big mistakes."

7.18

【原　文】

子所雅言，《诗》、《书》、执礼，皆雅言也。

【汉　译】

先生有用雅言的时候，如读《诗经》、《尚书》和行礼时，都必用雅言。

【英　译】

The Master used the correct Chinese pronunciation while reading *the Odes, the Book of History* and performing the rites.

7.19

【原　文】

叶公问孔子于子路，子路不对。子曰："女奚不曰：其为人也，发愤忘食，乐以忘忧，不知老之将至云尔。"

【汉　译】

叶公向子路问孔子是什么样的人，子路一时难以回答。先生说："你何不这样说：他这个人呀，发愤用功，连吃饭都给忘了，内心高兴时把忧愁都忘了，甚至连自己快老了也不知道，这样说就行了。"

【英　译】

The governor of She town asked Zi Lu about his Master. Zi Lu could not answer. Then the Master said, "Why not answer him just like this: He is the sort of man who is so absorbed in learning that he forgets to eat, who is so joyful that he forgets his worries, and who is even unaware of his old age approaching. That's it."

7.20

【原　文】

子曰：“我非生而知之者，好古，敏以求之者也。”

【汉　译】

孔子说：“我不是生来便知一切的，我是喜好古代文化，是靠勤奋求得的。”

【英　译】

The Master said, "I was not born knowledgeable but, loving the ancient culture, I am quick to learn it."

7.21

【原　文】

子不语：怪、力、乱、神。

【汉　译】

孔子不谈论怪异、强力、叛乱、鬼神这四样事情。

【英　译】

The Master did not talk about monstrosities, force, insurrection, ghosts and deities.

7.22

【原　文】

子曰：“三人行，必有我师焉；择其善者而从之，其不善者而改之。”

【汉　译】

孔子说："三人同行，其中必有可为我师者，选其善德而学习，其有不善的，我当引以为戒，进而自我改正。"

【英　译】

The Master said, "When three of us are walking, there must be one man who can be my teacher. I'd like to learn from his practical benevolence. As for his unkind action, I will learn a lesson from it and make self-correction."

7.23

【原　文】

子曰："天生德于予，桓魋其如予何？"

【汉　译】

孔子说："上天赋予了我这些品德，桓魋又能把我怎么样呢？"

【英　译】

The Master said, "It is Heaven that conferred the virtues upon me. What can Huan Tui do to me?"

(According to tradition, this was said on the occasion when Huan Tui, the Minister of War in Song, attempted to kill him.)

7.24

【原　文】

子曰："二三子以我为隐乎？吾无隐乎尔。吾无行而不与二三子者，是丘也。"

【汉　译】

孔子说："弟子们，你们以为我有什么可隐瞒的吗？我对你们没什么可隐瞒的。我没什么事不可以告诉你们的，这就是我孔丘的为人。"

【英　译】

The Master said, "My friends, do you think that I've kept something secret from you? Actually, there is nothing concealed from you. I have everything known to all of you. That's your Master Qiu."

7.25

【原　文】

子以四教：文、行、忠、信。

【汉　译】

先生从四个方面教人：典籍遗文、道德实践、为人忠诚、恪守信用。

【英　译】

The Master taught his disciples in four respects: documents and historical records, practical virtue, faithfulness and trustworthiness.

7.26

【原　文】

子曰："圣人，吾不得而见之矣；得见君子者，斯可矣。"
子曰："善人，吾不得而见之矣；得见有恒者，斯可矣。亡而为有，虚而为盈，约而为泰，难乎有恒矣。"

【汉　译】

孔子说："圣人，我是看不到了，能见到君子，也就可以了。"
孔子又说："善人，我是看不到了，能看到有操守的人就行了。没有却要装着有，空虚却要装着充实，穷困却要装作富足，这样的人难以保持好操守。"

【英　译】

The Master said, "It's impossible for me to see a sage. I shall feel contented if I meet a gentleman."

The Master said, "It's impossible for me to see a benevolent man. I will feel satisfied if I meet a man who is morally good. It's difficult for him to keep virtuous, as for a man who claims to have something when he has nothing, to be full when he is empty, and to be rich when he is poor."

7.27

【原　文】

子钓而不纲，弋不射宿。

【汉　译】

孔子只用鱼竿钓鱼，却不用大绳拉网捕鱼；孔子也射鸟，但不射归巢歇宿之鸟。

【英　译】

The Master caught fish with just a fishhook but not a fishnet, and he was shooting at only flying birds but not at the roosting birds.

7.28

【原　文】

子曰："盖有不知而作之者，我无是也。多闻，择其善者而从之；多见而识之。知之次也。"

【汉　译】

孔子说："大概有自己不懂却贸然行事的人吧，我是不会这样的。多听，选择其中好的加以接受；多看，都记在心上。这种求知方法仅次于生而知之。"

【英　译】

The Master said, "There are presumably some men who act recklessly without knowing. But I will not make such a fault. On the one hand, I open my eyes widely and learn from the humane actions. On the other hand, I observe more and bear all the details in mind. That's inferior to being born with knowledge."

7.29

【原　文】

　　互乡难与言，童子见，门人惑。子曰："与其进也，不与其退也，唯何甚？人洁己以进，与其洁也，不保其往也。"

【汉　译】

　　互乡这地方的人很难与之交谈，孔子却接见了当地一位少年，弟子们都感到疑惑不解。孔子说："我只赞许他的进步，不赞许他的退步。何必过分呢？人家改好了以求进步，就要赞许他能改正错误，不要死抓住他的过去不放。"

【英　译】

　　It was difficult to talk to the inhabitants of Hu Xiang who didn't behave themselves well. However, the Master held an interview with a boy from there, and therefore his disciples were puzzled. And then the Master said, "I only affirm his present progress, but not approve of his past mistakes. Why should we make such great demands? As they've corrected their own mistakes, we should regard their progress with favor but not mention their past deficiencies any longer."

7.30

【原　文】

　　子曰："仁远乎哉？我欲仁，斯仁至矣。"

【汉　译】

　　孔子说："难道仁德离我们很远吗？只要我想求仁，仁就会来。"

【英　译】

　　The Master said, "Is benevolence very far way from us? As long as I want to seek benevolence, it is bound to come afterwards."

7.31

【原　文】

　　陈司败问："昭公知礼乎？"孔子曰："知礼。"

　　孔子退，揖巫马期而进之，曰："吾闻君子不党，君子亦党乎？君取于吴，为同姓，谓之吴孟子。君而知礼，孰不知礼？"

　　巫马期以告。子曰："丘也幸，苟有过，人必知之。"

【汉　译】

　　陈司败向孔子问道："鲁昭公知礼吗？" 孔子说："他是知礼的。"

　　孔子走后，陈司败向巫马期作个揖，请他靠近自己，然后对他说："我听说君子从不偏袒别人，难道孔子还会包庇人吗？鲁国国君从吴国娶了位夫人，和国君同姓，称她为吴孟子。要是鲁君算得上知礼，还有谁不知礼呢？"

　　巫马期把这话告诉了孔子。孔子说："我是很幸运的，如果有错，人家一定会知道。"

【英　译】

Chen Sibai asked, "Is Duke Lu Zhao well versed in the rites?" The Master said, "Yes, he is."

After the Master left, Chen Sibai bowed to Wu Maqi and asked him to come near and said, "I have heard that gentleman should not be partially. Does the Master show partiality? The lord of the state Lu married a woman in the state Wu who is of the same clan bearing the name Ji as himself and afterwards he calls her as Wu Mengtzu. If the Lord Zhao knows the rites, will there be anyone who doesn't know?"

After Wu Maqi told this to him, the Master said, "I am really a fortunate man. If I make any mistakes, others are sure to know."

7.32

【原　文】

子与人歌而善，必使反之，而后和之。

【汉　译】

孔子和别人唱歌时，如果别人唱得好，一定请他再唱一遍，然后和他一起唱。

【英　译】

While singing with others, if a song was found attractive, the Master was bound to ask the singer to sing it again before participating in.

7.33

【原　文】

子曰："文，莫吾犹人也。躬行君子，则吾未之有得。"

【汉　译】

孔子说："仅就书本知识来说，大概我与别人差不多。要做一个身体力行的君子，我还没有达到。"

【英　译】

The Master said, "As far as book knowledge is concerned, presumably I can be the same with others. However, I haven't reached the standard as for being a practicing gentleman."

7.34

【原　文】

子曰："若圣与仁，则吾岂敢？抑为之不厌，诲人不倦，则可谓云尔已矣。"公西华曰："正唯弟子不能学也。"

【汉 译】

孔子说："若说圣与仁，我怎么敢当？只不过在这方面我能不厌烦地学习，而且教导别人也从不倦怠，就只算得上这些罢了。"公西华说："这正是我们弟子们所学不到的呀。"

【英 译】

The Master said, "How can I be worthy of a sage and benevolent man? Yet, in this respect can I learn without being tired and teach others without growing weary. That's it." Gong Xihua said, "This is exactly what we disciples are unable to learn from you."

7.35

【原 文】

子疾病，子路请祷。子曰："有诸？"子路对曰："有之。诔曰：'祷尔于上下神祇。'"子曰："丘之祷久矣。"

【汉 译】

孔子病得很重，子路请求向鬼神祈祷。孔子问道："有这回事吗？"子路答道："有这回事，《诔》文上说：'替你向天地神灵祷告。'"孔子说："我早已祈祷过了。"

【英 译】

The Master was seriously ill, and Zi Lu prayed for him. The Master said, "Is there such a thing?" Zi Lu said, "Yes. The text of Lei says, 'Say prayer for you to the gods of heaven and earth.'" The Master said, "I've been praying for a long time."

7.36

【原 文】

子曰："奢则不孙，俭则固。与其不孙也，宁固。"

【汉 译】

孔子说："奢侈就显得骄纵，节俭就显得寒酸。与其骄纵，宁可寒酸。"

【英 译】

The Master said, "Extravagance breeds arrogance; economy incurs shabbiness and misery. I would rather be shabby than arrogant."

7.37

【原 文】

子曰："君子坦荡荡，小人长戚戚。"

【汉 译】

孔子说："君子总是心胸宽广，小人常是局促忧伤。"

【英 译】

The Master said, "A gentleman is always broad-minded, while a small man is usually full of anxiety."

7.38

【原 文】

子温而厉，威而不猛，恭而安。

【汉 译】

孔子温和而又严肃，威严而不凶猛，恭敬而又安舒。

【英 译】

The Master is gentle yet stern, dignified yet ferocious, and respectful yet feeling at ease.

泰伯篇第八

8.1

【原　文】

子曰："泰伯，其可谓至德也已矣。三以天下让，民无得而称焉。"

【汉　译】

孔子说："可以说，泰伯的品德是极其高尚的。他几次把天下让给季历，老百姓真不知道用什么语言来赞美他。"

【英　译】

The Master said, "Tai Bo can be said to be an extremely virtuous man. He renounced the right of succession of the sovereign lord several times. Therefore, the common people were unable to find the appropriate words for praising his virtues."

8.2

【原　文】

子曰："恭而无礼则劳，慎而无礼则葸，勇而无礼则乱，直而无礼则绞。君子笃于亲，则民兴于仁；故旧不遗，则民不偷。"

【汉　译】

孔子说："恭敬却不知礼，就会劳苦不安；谨慎却不知礼，便会畏惧胆怯；勇敢而不知礼，就会犯上作乱；直率而不知礼，便会出语尖刻刺人。在上位的人若能真心爱护其亲属，老百姓就会崇尚仁德；在上位的人若能不遗弃他的故旧，老百姓便不会对人冷漠无情。"

【英　译】

The Master said, "A man will wear out if he is respectful without knowing the spirit of rites; a man will become timid if he is cautious without knowing the spirit of rites; a man will offend his superiors and make trouble if he is brave without knowing the spirit of rites; a man will be vey caustic about others if he is straightforward without knowing the spirit of rites. If a gentleman feels great affection for his kinsfolk, the common people will be encouraged to worship and believe in virtue and morality. If a gentleman does not desert his old friends and acquaintances, the common people will not become indifferent to the suffering of others."

8.3

【原　文】

曾子有疾，召门弟子曰：“启予足！启予手！《诗》云：‘战战兢兢，如临深渊，如履薄冰。’而今而后，吾知免夫！小子！”

【汉　译】

曾子生病了，把弟子们召到身边说：“看看我的脚，看看我的手，都好好的吧！《诗经》上说：‘小心呀！谨慎呀！就像站在深潭旁边，就像行走在薄冰上面。’从今以后，我知道自己可以免遭祸害了，弟子们哪！”

【英　译】

Zeng Zi was seriously ill and he summoned his disciples and said, "Take a look at my hands, and take a look at my feet. *The Odes* say, 'In fear trembling as if approaching a deep chasm, and as if walking on thin ice.' From now on, I can be spared of penalty and havoc, my dear friends."

8.4

【原　文】

　　曾子有疾，孟敬子问之。曾子言曰："鸟之将死，其鸣也哀；人之将死，其言也善。君子所贵乎道者三：动容貌，斯远暴慢矣；正颜色，斯近信矣；出辞气，斯远鄙倍矣。笾豆之事，则有司存。"

【汉　译】

　　曾子生病了，孟敬子去看望他。曾子说："鸟临死时的叫声是悲哀的；人快死时说的话是善意的。君子重视道有三方面：能注意自己的容貌庄重，就可以避免粗暴；能常注意脸色严肃，就可以使自己接近诚信；能常注意说话的言辞语气，就可以避免粗野悖理。至于祭祀和礼仪细节的事，自有管事小吏负责！"

【英　译】

　　Zeng Zi was seriously ill and Meng Jingzi visited him. Zeng Zi said, "A dying bird cries sadly; a dying man says his words kindly. A gentleman should value the Way in three respects: a solemn countenance can avoid rudeness; a serious expression comes close to honesty; a proper tone in speaking can refrain him from being offensive and going against common sense. As for the matter of sacrifice and rites, there are certainly some officials to manage."

8.5

【原　文】

　　曾子曰："以能问于不能，以多问于寡；有若无，实若虚，犯而不校。昔者吾友尝从事于斯矣。"

【汉　译】

　　曾子说："自己有才能，却向没才能的人请教；自己学识丰富，却向学识浅薄的人请教；自己有学问，却像没有学问一样；自己满腹知识，却像空无所有一样；被人冒犯，自己也不计较。从前我的朋友就曾这样做了。"

【英　译】

Zeng Zi said, "A capable man yet asks the advice from an incapable one; a learned man yet consults a superficial one; a man full of knowledge yet appears to be wanting; a man of great learning acts as if he has nothing at all; a man never bothers about someone who offends him. A friend of mine ever conducted like this in former times."

8.6

【原　文】

曾子曰："可以托六尺之孤，可以寄百里之命，临大节而不可夺也。君子人与？君子人也。"

【汉　译】

曾子说："可以把幼主托付给他，可以把江山社稷交付给他，面对生死关头却不动摇屈服。这样的人称得上是君子吗？当然是君子啊！"

【英　译】

Zeng Zi said, "A man is so dependable that you can leave an orphan to him, and that you can entrust the state to him. Moreover, he is not yielding in the vital moment of life and death. Is such a man called a gentleman? Certainly he is."

8.7

【原　文】

曾子曰："士不可以不弘毅，任重而道远。仁以为己任，不亦重乎？死而后已，不亦远乎？"

【汉　译】

曾子说："读书人不可以不弘大刚毅，因为他们肩负的责任重大，而且道路遥远。以求仁为己任，难道这不重大吗？到死方休，难道说不遥远吗?"

【英　译】

　　Zeng Zi said, "A scholar must be resolute and steadfast, for he bears the heavy burden and takes the long road. He regards seeking benevolence as his obligation. Isn't it significant?　He does not stop to search for benevolence until death. Isn't it long?"

8.8

【原　文】

　　子曰:"兴于诗,立于礼,成于乐。"

【汉　译】

　　孔子说:"修养始于学诗,自立于学礼,完成于学乐。"

【英　译】

　　The Master said, "Accomplishment in self-cultivation starts from learning poems, earns one's own living from learning rites, and is completed through learning music."

8.9

【原　文】

　　子曰:"民可使由之,不可使知之。"

【汉　译】

　　孔子说:"只能使老百姓照着我们的意思去做,不可使他们懂得为什么要这样做。"

【英　译】

　　The Master said, "You can only let the common people follow a policy, but should not let them know why."

8.10

【原　文】

子曰："好勇疾贫，乱也。人而不仁，疾之已甚，乱也。"

【汉　译】

孔子说："好勇而又恨自己贫穷，这样的人就会作乱。对不仁之人憎恨过分，也会出乱子。"

【英　译】

The Master said, "If he is fond of being brave but detests poverty, a man may cause trouble. If he hates an evil man too bitterly, he can also commit an offence."

8.11

【原　文】

子曰："如有周公之才之美，使骄且吝，其余不足观也已。"

【汉　译】

孔子说："一个人即使有周公那样美好的才能，如果他又骄傲又小气，那他其他方面也就不值得一看了。"

【英　译】

The Master said, "Even if a man were as gifted as the Duke of Zhou, the rest of this character would not be appreciated if he was either arrogant or mean."

8.12

【原　文】

子曰："三年学，不至于谷，不易得也。"

【汉　译】

孔子说："读书三年，依然不想做官，此人难得呀！"

【英 译】

The Master said, "It's difficult to find a man who has studied for three years but does not try to seek an official post."

8.13

【原 文】

子曰:"笃信好学,守死善道。危邦不入,乱邦不居。天下有道则见,无道则隐。邦有道,贫且贱焉,耻也。邦无道,富且贵焉,耻也。"

【汉 译】

孔子说:"坚守诚信,努力学习,固守善道,至死不渝。政局危险的国家不去,政局动乱的国家不住。天下太平就出来做官,天下混乱则韬光养晦。国家政治清明,自己依然贫贱,这是可耻的;国家政治黑暗,而自己却富贵,也是可耻的。"

【英 译】

The Master said, "Keep trustworthy and be fond of learning, and stick to the good way until one's death. Do not enter a state which is in danger; do not stay in a state which is in disturbance. Go out to search for an official post under good governance; conceal one's own capacities if government corruption. It is shameful for one to be poor and humble when the Way prevails in the state. Similarly, it is shameful for one to be rich and noble when the Way is not predominant in the state."

8.14

【原 文】

子曰:"不在其位,不谋其政。"

【汉 译】

孔子说:"不在那个职位上,就不要考虑那个职位上的事。"

【英　译】

The Master said, "You should not be concerned about its government affairs unless you occupy the post."

8.15

【原　文】

子曰："师挚之始，《关雎》之乱，洋洋乎盈耳哉！"

【汉　译】

孔子说："从太师挚开始演奏序曲，一直到结尾合奏《关雎》，丰富美妙的音乐之声充盈了我的耳房啊！"

【英　译】

The Master said, "Mr. Zhi, the Master Musician, played the music from the prelude to the coda of *Guan Ju*, i.e. the first ode in *the Odes*. My ears are filled with the rich and beautiful sound."

8.16

【原　文】

子曰："狂而不直，侗而不愿，悾悾而不信，吾不知之矣。"

【汉　译】

孔子说："狂妄而不率直，无知而不谨慎，表面诚实却不守信，我真不知道这种人会这样子。"

【英　译】

The Master said, "There are some men who are frenzied but not straightforward, ignorant but not cautious, outwardly honest but trustworthy. I really don't know why they behave like this."

8.17

【原　文】

子曰："学如不及，犹恐失之。"

【汉　译】

孔子说："求学好似追逐猎物似地唯恐赶不上，赶上了又怕失去。"

【英　译】

The Master said, "Seeking knowledge is just like chasing a prey. You always worry about how to catch up with it. Yet when you got it, you fear that you might lose it in time."

8.18

【原　文】

子曰："巍巍乎，舜禹之有天下也，而不与焉！"

【汉　译】

孔子说："多么伟大啊！舜和禹虽拥有天下，却不为自己谋私利。"

【英　译】

The Master said, "How lofty they are! Yao and Shun were in possession of the state, but they didn't seize power by violence."

8.19

【原　文】

子曰："大哉，尧之为君也！巍巍乎！唯天为大，唯尧则之。荡荡乎！民无能名焉。巍巍乎其有成功也！焕乎其有文章！"

【汉　译】

　　孔子说："尧这样的君主，真伟大啊！多么崇高啊！天是最高大的，唯有尧可以与天相比。多么广大呀！民众真不知道该如何称赞他。他那时的功绩太高大啦！他所指定的礼仪制度多么光明美好呀！"

【英　译】

The Master said, "What a great lord Yao was! How lofty! Only heaven is the vastest one, and only Yao could model himself on it. His favor was so boundless that the common people really didn't know how to praise him. What his outstanding merits and achievements! What his brilliant proprieties!"

8.20

【原　文】

　　舜有臣五人而天下治。武王曰："予有乱臣十人。"孔子曰："才难，不其然乎？唐虞之际，于斯为盛。有妇人焉，九人而已。三分天下有其二，以服事殷。周之德，其可谓至德也已矣。"

【汉　译】

　　舜有贤臣五人而天下大治。周武王说："我有治国之臣十人。"孔子说："人才难得，不是这样吗？唐尧和虞舜时期比周武王那个时候人才最兴盛。但其中还有一位是妇人，所以只有九人而已。周文王得了天下的三分之二，还继续服侍殷商，周朝的道德可以说是最高了。"

【英　译】

Shun had five worthy courtiers to help him, and therefore the country was well governed. King Wu said, "I have ten worthy courtiers to assist me in governing a country." The Master commented, "It's difficult to come by the talented people, isn't it? There was the largest number of talented people during the period between Yao dynasty and Shun dynasty as well as the governing period of King Wu. However, there was a female courtier among his ten talented people, and as a matter of fact King Wu only had nine courtiers. Zhou dynasty continued to serve Yin dynasty when the lord Zhou was in possession of two thirds of the whole Empire; therefore, its morality can be said to be the loftiest."

8.21

【原　文】

子曰：“禹，吾无间然矣。菲饮食而致孝乎鬼神，恶衣服而致美乎黻冕，卑宫室而尽力乎沟洫。禹，吾无间然矣。”

【汉　译】

孔子说：“对于禹，我没有可批评的了。他自己饮食菲薄却尽力孝敬鬼神，他自己衣服破旧却尽量着华美的祭服，他自己宫室低矮却致力兴修水利。对于禹，我没有什么可批评的了。”

【英　译】

The Master said, "I can find no fault with Yu. He went through a thrifty and poor life but he did his best to serve the ancestral spirits and ghosts. He ordinarily wore the old and shabby clothes but he tried his best to wear the splendid robes and caps on sacrificial occasions. He lived in the low and humble palace but he devoted himself to the building of irrigation canals. As for Yu, I can find no fault with him."

子罕篇第九

9.1

【原　文】

子罕言利，与命与仁。

【汉　译】

孔子平日很少谈利，而赞同天命和仁德。

【英　译】

The Master rarely talked about profit, but he had a high regard for destiny and benevolence.

9.2

【原　文】

达巷党人曰："大哉孔子！博学而无所成名。"子闻之，谓门弟子曰："吾何执？执御乎？执射乎？吾执御矣。"

【汉　译】

达巷的党人说："孔子真伟大啊！他学问广博，却没有成名的专长。"孔子听了这话，对他的弟子们说："我该专心于哪一项技艺呢？是驾车呢？还是射箭吗？我想还是驾车吧。"

【英　译】

Some people from Da Xiang village said, "What a great man Confucius is! He has a great deal of extensive and profound knowledge, but he has not made a name for himself in any special field." After hearing of this, the Master said to his disciples, "What specialty should I work for? Is it driving or archery? I think I'd prefer driving."

9.3

【原　文】

子曰："麻冕，礼也；今也纯，俭，吾从众。拜下，礼也；今拜乎上，泰也。虽违众，吾从下。"

【汉　译】

孔子说："用麻冕是符合古礼的，现在改用黑丝做冕，比用麻冕节省了，我赞同大家的做法。臣见君，先在堂下拜，再升堂拜，这是合乎传统的礼的；现在大家都只在堂上拜了，我觉得这样太骄纵了。虽然违逆于大家的做法，我还是主张先在堂下拜。"

【英　译】

The Master said, "A hat made of linen is what is prescribed by the rites. Today a hat is made of black silk instead, and this is more frugal. Accordingly, I prefer to follow the majority. When a courtier calling on the lord, he should firstly prostrate himself before ascending the steps of the palace and then do it again in the upper hall. This is what is prescribed by the rites. Today people prostrate themselves in just upper hall of the palace, and I think their actions are too arrogant. Although being against the popular conventions, I still insist on prostrating myself before ascending the steps of palace."

9.4

【原　文】

子绝四：毋意，毋必，毋固，毋我。

【汉　译】

孔子杜绝了这四种毛病：不主观臆测，不绝对肯定，不固执己见，不唯我独尊。

【英　译】

The Master was freed of the four defects: making subjective judgments, making arbitrary decisions, being obstinate, considering oneself not the Way.

9.5

【原　文】

子畏于匡，曰："文王既没，文不在兹乎？天之将丧斯文也，后死者不得与于斯文也；天之未丧斯文也，匡人其如予何？"

【汉　译】

孔子在匡地被拘禁，他说："文王死后，古代文化遗产不都在我这里吗？上天若消除这种文化，我也不会掌握这些文化了；上天若不消除这种文化，那匡人又能把我怎么样呢？"

【英　译】

When being imprisoned in Kuang, the Master said, "After the death of Lord Wen, isn't the cultural heritage preserved in me? If Heaven intends to destroy this culture, I will not be able to master it. If Heaven doesn't want to, what can the people of Kuang do to me?"

9.6

【原　文】

太宰问于子贡曰："夫子圣者与？何其多能也？"子贡曰："固天纵之将圣，又多能也。"子闻之，曰："太宰知我乎！吾少也贱，故多能鄙事。君子多乎哉？不多也。"

【汉　译】

太宰问子贡说："你们先生是圣人吗？为什么这样多才多艺呢？"子贡说："是上天使他成为圣人，又让他多才多艺的。"

孔子听说后，说："太宰了解我呀！我小时候贫贱，所以能做很多卑贱的技艺。君子有这么多能吗？不多的呀！"

【英　译】

Tai Zai asked Zi Gong, "Is your Master is a sage? Why is he so versatile?" Zi Gong said, "It's Heaven that made him a sage and versatile man."

On hearing of this, the Master said, "How well Tai Zai knows me! I was poor and humble when I was young. That is the reason why I am skilled in many menial things. Is a gentleman really skilled in many things? No, not at all."

9.7

【原　文】

牢曰："子云：'吾不试，故艺。'"

【汉　译】

牢说："孔子说过：'因我没有被大用，所以学得许多技艺。'"

【英　译】

Lao said, "The Master said, 'I have never been employed in important position, so I can master many skills.'"

9.8

【原　文】

子曰："吾有知乎哉？无知也。有鄙夫问于我，空空如也。我叩其两端而竭焉。"

【汉　译】

孔子说："我有知识吗？我实在是无知啊。有个农人问我问题，我什么也不知道。我就从他所提问题的两端来问他，一步步问到底就是了。"

【英 译】

The Master said, "Do I really have knowledge? No, I do not. Once a farmer asked me one question, but I couldn't answer it. And afterwards I kept working hard at the two sides of the question until I got everything out of it."

9.9

【原 文】

子曰："凤鸟不至，河不出图，吾已矣夫!"

【汉 译】

孔子说："凤凰飞不来了，黄河不出现龙背八卦图了，我这一辈子也就完了。"

【英 译】

The Master said, "Neither the phoenix appears nor the Yellow River displays its Chart (Both the Phoenix and the Chart were auspicious omens). It's impossible for me to witness an era of prosperity."

9.10

【原 文】

子见齐衰者、冕衣裳者与瞽者，见之，虽少，必作；过之，必趋。

【汉 译】

孔子见到穿丧服的、穿着贵族服装的以及眼瞎的人，见面的时候，即使他们是年轻人，孔子也要从坐席上起身；从他们身旁走过，一定要快步走。

【英 译】

While meeting the men who were in mourning for their relatives or wearing ceremonial caps and robes or blind, the Master would rise to his feet on seeing them, though they were young; and whenever passing by them, he would quicken his steps as a sign of respect.

9.11

【原　文】

颜渊喟然叹曰："仰之弥高，钻之弥坚。瞻之在前，忽焉在后。夫子循循然善诱之，博我以文，约我以礼，欲罢不能。既竭吾才，如有所立卓尔。虽欲从之，末由也已。"

【汉　译】

颜渊感叹道："老师的学问道德，我抬头仰望，愈看愈觉得高；我努力去钻研它，越钻研越觉得深。看见它好像在前面，忽而又到了后面。老师循循善诱教导我，用文献知识丰富我，用礼来约束我的行为，使我无法停止学习。我虽已竭尽全力，它好像仍然矗立在我眼前，高不可攀。"

【英　译】

After heaving a sigh, Yan Yuan said, "The more I look up at the Master's learning and virtue, the higher it appears. The more intensively I study it, the more profound it becomes. I see it before me, but suddenly it goes behind. The Master was good at instructing me step by step; he broadened me with culture and knowledge of documentation; he restrained me with proprieties and rules. It is impossible for me to abandon learning from him. In spite of having done all I can, his learning and virtue appears to rise sheer above me, and it's difficult for me to scale the height of it."

9.12

【原　文】

子疾病，子路使门人为臣。病间，曰："久矣哉，由之行诈也！无臣而为有臣。吾谁欺？欺天乎？且予与其死于臣之手也，无宁死于二三子之手乎？且予纵不得大葬，予死于道路乎？"

【汉 译】

孔子病重，子路就派孔子的门人做家臣为孔子料理后事。孔子病情好转后，说道：“仲由很久以来就弄虚作假啊！我没有家臣，却要装着有家臣，我骗谁呢？骗天吗？我与其死在家臣手里，还不如死在你们这些弟子手里呢！这不更好吗？况且，我纵使没条件享受大夫的葬礼，难道我会死在路边没人安葬吗？”

【英 译】

The Master was gravely ill. Zi Lu sent the Master's disciple to serve him as a butler. After his illness improved, the Master said, "Zi Lu has been practicing deception like this for a long time. It's obvious that I don't have any butlers at all, but pretend to have. Whom do we deceive? Deceiving Heaven? To be frank, I'd rather die in your hands rather than die in a butler. Isn't it better? In addition, even if I were not given a funeral of a senior official, isn't it possible that I was dying by the roadside?"

9.13

【原 文】

子贡曰：“有美玉于斯，韫椟而藏诸？求善贾而沽诸？”子曰：“沽之哉！沽之哉！我待贾者也。”

【汉 译】

子贡说：“有一块美玉在这里，是把它放在柜子里收藏起来呢，还是找个识货的商人把它卖掉呢？”孔子说：“卖掉！卖掉！我在等待识货的人呢！”

【英 译】

Zi Gong said, "Here is a piece of beautiful jade. Keep it in a cupboard or find a knowledgeable trader to sell it?" The Master said, "Of course sell it! Of course sell it! I'm just waiting for a knowledgeable trader who is capable to judge it."

9.14

【原　文】

子欲居九夷。或曰："陋，如之何？"子曰："君子居之，何陋之有？"

【汉　译】

孔子想到东方去居住。有人说："那地方很闭塞落后，怎么好住呢？"孔子说："君子去居住，还会有什么闭塞呢？"

【英　译】

The Master intended to settle in a remote eastern place of China. Someone said, "How can you live there as the place is very backward and isolated?"

The Master said, "Since a gentleman settles among them, how can it be backward and isolated?"

9.15

【原　文】

子曰："吾自卫反鲁，然后乐正，《雅》《颂》各得其所。"

【汉　译】

孔子说："我从卫国回到鲁国后，才把乐曲的音律整理好，使《雅》乐与《颂》乐各自归于它们应有的位置。"

【英　译】

The Master said, "Tuning pitch-pipes and modes of music were put right after I returned from the state Wei to the state Lu. And the music *ya* and the music *song* in *the Odes* have also been assigned their proper places."

9.16

【原　文】

　　子曰："出则事公卿，入则事父兄，丧事不敢不勉，不为酒困，何有于我哉？"

【汉　译】

　　孔子说："出外侍奉公卿，在家侍奉父兄，办丧事不敢不尽心尽力，不被酒所困扰，这些对我来说有何困难呢？"

【英　译】

　　The Master said, "Serve the high officials away from home, support my parents and elder brothers at home, exert my utmost efforts in arranging funerals, and not let drink spoil anything. How can it be difficult for me to do all these?"

9.17

【原　文】

　　子在川上曰："逝者如斯夫！不舍昼夜。"

【汉　译】

　　孔子站在河边说："时光流逝，就像这河水一样啊！它日夜不停地向前流去。"

【英　译】

　　While standing on a river side, the Master said, "Time elapses just like the flowing water in the river. It is running forward night and day."

9.18

【原　文】

　　子曰："吾未见好德如好色者也。"

【汉　译】

孔子说："我没见过能像爱美色那样爱好德的人。"

【英　译】

The Master said, "I've never met a man who loves virtue as much as he loves beauty in women."

9.19

【原　文】

子曰："譬如为山，未成一篑，止，吾止也。譬如平地，虽覆一篑，进，吾往也。"

【汉　译】

孔子说："譬如堆土成山，只差一筐土就堆成了，却停下了，是我自己要停的。又譬如在平地上，虽然只倒下了一筐土，如果继续干下去，也是我自己坚持干下去的。"

【英　译】

The Master said, "As in the case of making a mound, I failed to accomplish the job because of lacking the very last basketful earth, and it's my own decision. As in the case of tipping only one basketful earth on the flat ground, I continue to do like this, and it's my own decision that I persist in doing it."

9.20

【原　文】

子曰："语之而不惰者，其回也与！"

【汉　译】

孔子说："听我讲话而毫不懈怠的，大概只有颜回吧！"

【英 译】

The Master said, "I suppose, it is only Yan Hui who doggedly listened to my speech."

9.21

【原 文】

子谓颜渊，曰："惜乎！吾见其进也，未见其止也。"

【汉 译】

孔子谈到颜渊时，说道："可惜呀！他死早了，我只见他不断进步，从未见他止步不前。"

【英 译】

While talking about Yan Yuan, the Master said, "What a pity! He passed away at the young age. I've watched him make progress, but I did not see him go no further."

9.22

【原 文】

子曰："苗而不秀者有矣夫！秀而不实者有矣夫！"

【汉 译】

孔子说："庄稼长出了苗而不能吐穗扬花的情况是有的！吐穗开花了而不结果实的情形也是有的！"

【英 译】

The Master said, "There are crops that have seedlings without producing blossoms, and there are also crops that have blossoms without producing fruits."

9.23

【原 文】

子曰:"后生可畏,焉知来者之不如今也? 四十、五十而无闻焉,斯亦不足畏也已。"

【汉 译】

孔子说:"年轻人是可怕的,哪能知道后一辈的就不如现在这一辈人呢? 若一个人到了四五十岁还默默无闻,那他就不值得敬畏了。"

【英 译】

The Master said, "It is proper that we should treat the young with awe. How can we know that the following generation is not as good as the present one? If a man is still unknown to all at the age of forty or fifty, then he does not deserve to be held in awe."

9.24

【原 文】

子曰:"法语之言,能无从乎? 改之为贵。巽与之言,能无说乎? 绎之为贵。说而不绎,从而不改,吾未如之何也已矣。"

【汉 译】

孔子说:"合乎礼法的正言规劝,能不接受吗? 只有改正了错误才是可贵的。恭敬赞许的话,听了能不高兴吗? 能分析鉴别其真意才是可贵的。只管高兴而不分析其真意,一味听从而不改正错误,对这种人我可就没有办法了。"

【英 译】

The Master said, "How can people not accept the exemplary words correspondent with the rules of proprieties? However, it's really admirable to correct the mistakes and reform oneself. How can people not feel happy after hearing the complimentary words? Yet, what's more important is that he is capable of probing into its true meaning. There is nothing I can do about the man who feels happy but does not analyze its true meaning or the man who gives agreement but does not rectify himself."

9.25

【原　文】

子曰："主忠信，毋友不如已者，过则勿惮改。"

【汉　译】

孔子说："人要以诚信为本，不要结交那些不如自己的朋友，有了过错不要怕改正。"

【英　译】

The Master said, "One must take honesty as his cardinal principle. Don't make friends with anyone who is not as good as you. Don't hesitate to correct it if you made a mistake."

9.26

【原　文】

子曰："三军可夺帅也，匹夫不可夺志也。"

【汉　译】

孔子说："三军之众，可以夺其主帅；匹夫之志，谁也夺不去。"

【英　译】

The Master said, "The There Armies are capable of depriving of their commander, but there is no way to deprive a common man of his aspiration."

9.27

【原　文】

子曰："衣敝缊袍，与衣狐貉者立，而不耻者，其由也与？'不忮不求，何用不臧？'"子路终身诵之。子曰："是道也，何足以臧？"

【汉 译】

孔子说："穿着破旧的丝绵袍，和穿着狐貉裘皮袍的人站在一起，却不感到羞耻的，大概也只有仲由吧!《诗经》上说'不嫉妒，不贪求，有什么不好呢?'"子路听后，从此常反复吟诵这两句诗。孔子又说："仅仅这样，又怎能算得上好了呢?"

【英 译】

The Master said, "It is perhaps only Zi Lu, dressed in a worn cotton-padded gown, who does not feel ashamed while standing side by side with a man wearing fox or badger fur overcoat. *The Odes* say, 'If he is neither jealous nor greedy, how can a man be anything but good?'" After hearing of this, Zi Lu constantly recited these verses repeatedly. The Master said again, "The way inferred from these verses will hardly enable one to be good."

9.28

【原 文】

子曰："岁寒，然后知松柏之后彫也。"

【汉 译】

孔子说："要到严寒的冬天，才知道松柏是最后凋谢的。"

【英 译】

The Master said, "Only when the cold winter comes can we know that the pine and the cypress are the last to wither away."

9.29

【原 文】

子曰："知者不惑，仁者不忧，勇者不惧。"

【汉 译】

孔子说："智者心无困惑，仁者心无忧虑，勇者心无畏惧。"

【英 译】

The Master said, "The wise never feel perplexed; the benevolent never feel worried; the valiant never feel afraid."

9.30

【原 文】

子曰："可与共学，未可与适道；可与适道，未可与立；可与立，未可与权。"

【汉 译】

孔子说："可以和他一起学习，但未必可以和他共同向道；可以和他共同向道，但未必可以和他一起坚守道；可以和他一起坚守道，但未必可以和他一道通权达变。"

【英 译】

The Master said, "Someone may be treated as a partner to learn together, yet you may not be in the pursuit of the Way with him; someone may be treated as a partner in the pursuit of the Way, yet you may not be able to stick to the Way with him; someone may be treated as a partner to stick to the Way, yet you may not be able to adapt yourself to circumstances together with him."

9.31

【原 文】

"唐棣之华，偏其反而。岂不尔思？室是远而。"子曰："未之思也，夫何远之有？"

【汉 译】

"棠棣花开，翩翩摇摆。我岂不思念你啊？只因家离得太远了。"孔子说："怕是没有想念吧！若真想念的话，还有什么远的呢？"

【英 译】

Here is an old poem saying, "O, Tang Di flowers! They're so lightly fluttering. Can it be said that I don't miss you? It's only because I live too far away from you." The Master said, "You did not really think of her. If you did, you would not care about the distance."

乡党篇第十

10.1

【原　文】

孔子于乡党，恂恂如也，似不能言者。其在宗庙朝廷，便便言，唯谨尔。

【汉　译】

孔子在乡里，显得谦虚恭顺，好像不会说话的样子。他在宗庙朝廷上，说话却清楚明白，只是很谨慎罢了。

【英　译】

While in the hometown, the Master was submissive and seemed unable to express himself clearly. In the ancestral temple and court, he was a man of great eloquence, yet he was very cautious in his speech.

10.2

【原　文】

朝，与下大夫言，侃侃如也；与上大夫言，訚訚如也。君在，踧踖如也，与与如也。

【汉　译】

孔子在朝廷，同下大夫交谈，温和而快乐；同上大夫交谈，和颜悦色而又直言争辩。君视朝时，孔子恭恭敬敬而又威仪适中，既不紧张，也不懈怠。

【英　译】

While staying at court, the Master talked with the lower rank officials pleasantly and gently, and he talked with the higher rank officials kindly and honestly. In the presence of his lord, the Master talked to the lord reverently and composedly.

10.3

【原　文】

　　君召使摈，色勃如也，足躩如也。揖所与立，左右手，衣前后，襜如也。趋进，翼如也。宾退，必复命曰："宾不顾矣。"

【汉　译】

　　国君召孔子做傧相，去接待宾客，孔子神色变得庄重，走路也快起来。他向同立的傧相作揖，向两边左右拱手，衣裳也跟着前后摆动，但整齐不乱。他由中庭快步向前时，其姿势如鸟舒翼好看。宾客走后，他必向君王回复说："客人不再回头了。"

【英　译】

　　When the lord summoned the Master to receive the guests, he appeared very serious and his pace became quick. While bowing to the ushers beside him with his hands folded, he waved his hand to the left and then to the right with his robe forward and backward rather neatly. He stepped forward quickly as though the bird were gliding on its wings. After the guests left, he was bound to report, "The guests will never turn round again."

10.4

【原　文】

　　入公门，鞠躬如也，如不容。
　　立不中门，行不履阈。
　　过位，色勃如也，足躩如也，其言似不足者。
　　摄齐升堂，鞠躬如也，屏气似不息者。
　　出，降一等，逞颜色，怡怡如也。

没阶，趋进，翼如也。

复其位，踧踖如也。

【汉　译】

孔子走进朝廷的门，非常恭敬而谨慎，好像没有容身之地。

站，不站在门中间；走，不踩住门槛。

经过君主座位时，神态恭敬庄重，脚步轻快，说话好像底气不足。

他提起衣服下摆上堂时，恭敬谨慎，敛身憋气，好像不呼吸一样。

退出了，下一级台阶，神态便舒展了，一副怡然自得的样子。

下完台阶，就快步向前走，像鸟儿舒翼一般。

回到自己的位置上，又显得恭敬而不安。

【英　译】

Entering his lord's court gate, the Master looked reverent and prudent as if there were no place to conceal him. When standing, he never occupied the centre of the gateway; when walking, he never stepped on the threshold. While passing by the lord's station, he looked earnestly and quickened his step, and spoke with a weak voice as if not to have strong lungs. When he raised his robe hem to ascend the hall, he appeared courteous and cautious, he held his breath as if he didn't breathe at all. When coming out and descending the next step, he seemed to be relaxing and no longer tense. When walking down all the steps, he went forward with quickened steps as a bird stretching its wings. After returning back to his seat, he still appeared differential but nervous.

10.5

【原　文】

执圭，鞠躬如也，如不胜。上如揖，下如授。勃如战色，足蹜蹜，如有循。享礼，有容色。私觌，愉愉如也。

【汉　译】

孔子出使邻国，手里举着圭，恭敬而谨慎，好像举不动似的。

执圭在上，好像和人作揖；在下，像是递东西给人。脸色显得庄重，战战兢兢，脚步细碎，好像脚下有物，要顺着它前行似的。献礼的时候，则和颜悦色。私下和君臣会见时，则显得轻松愉快。

【英　译】

When holding a piece of jade named Gui in his hand, the Master looked deferential and cautious as though he were unable to hold it. He held the jade upwards as though he made a bow; he held the jade downwards as though he were to pass a gift to others. He appeared solemn as if in fear and trembling, and his feet were constrained as if following as a straight line. When offering a gift, he looked genial. While having a private interview with the lord, he seemed relaxed and cheerful.

10.6

【原　文】

君子不以绀緅饰，红紫不以为亵服。

当暑，袗絺绤，必表而出之。

缁衣，羔裘；素衣，麑裘；黄衣，狐裘。

亵裘长，短右袂。

必有寝衣，长一身有半。

狐貉之厚以居。

去丧，无所不佩。

非帷裳，必杀之。

羔裘玄冠不以吊。

吉月，必朝服而朝。

【汉　译】

君子不用深青透红和黑里透红的布做衣服的镶边，不用红色和紫色的布来做家里穿的便服。

夏天，在室内穿葛布单衣，但外出时必穿外衣。

黑色罩衣配紫羔皮袍，白色罩衣配白鹿皮袍，黄色罩衣配狐皮袍。

平时在家穿的皮袄，较出门穿的衣服稍长，要把右袖裁短些。

夜里睡觉一定要穿寝衣，它有人一身半长。

冬天，用厚厚的狐貉皮做成坐垫。

丧事完后，衣带上可佩带各种玉器装饰物。

除非上朝和祭祀时穿的礼服，其余衣裳一定要裁边。

去吊丧时，不穿黑色羔裘，不戴黑色礼帽。

每年正月岁首，一定要穿着朝服去朝拜君主。

【英　译】

A gentleman should neither choose dark purple and maroon cloth to make hems nor use red and purple material to make informal dress.

In the heat of summer, he should wear the coarse unlined clothes and must wear the outer garment away from home.

The black outer garment should be matched with the purple lambskin underwear; the white outer garment should be matched with the white deerskin underwear; the yellow outer garment should be matched with the fox skin underwear.

His informal fur coat was a little bit longer, so the right sleeve should be cut relatively short.

He should wear a pair of pajamas at night, of which the length should be one and a half that of his height.

The thick fox and raccoon furs are selected to make the seat cushions in winter.

After the funeral, he may be allowed to wear all sorts of jade ornaments.

Apart from the clothes for attending a sovereign's court and sacrificial rites, the other clothes must have the hems cut.

The black lamb fur coats and black hats should not be worn on visits of condolence.

On New Year's Day, he must wear the court dress to pay homage to his sovereign in court.

10.7

【原　文】

齐，必有明衣，布。齐必变食，居必迁坐。

【汉　译】

遇斋戒沐浴时，一定要有浴衣，用布做成。

斋戒时，一定要改变日常饮食，也要改变平时居处。

【英　译】

On fast days, he must wear the bathrobe made of cloth. During fast period, he should change to a very simple diet and not live in his habitual residence at home.

10.8

【原　文】

食不厌精，脍不厌细。

食饐而餲，鱼馁而肉败，不食。色恶，不食。臭恶，不食。失饪，不食。不时，不食。割不正，不食。不得其酱，不食。

肉虽多，不使胜食气。

唯酒无量，不及乱。

沽酒市脯，不食。

不撤姜食，不多食。

【汉　译】

米不因舂得精而多食，肉不因切得细而多吃。

食物经久腐败变味，鱼和肉腐烂变坏，都不吃。食物颜色变了，也不吃。气味变了，也不吃。烹饪得不好，也不吃。不当时的，也不吃。肉割得不合常规，也不吃。调味品不合适的，也不吃。

席上肉虽多，但吃的量不得超过饭食。

唯有饮酒不限量，但也不能喝醉。

从集市上买来的酒和肉干不吃。

吃完饭了，姜不撤掉，但也不多吃。

【英 译】

He should not eat his fill of polished rice, nor should he eat his fill of finely minced meat.

He should not eat moldy rice, nor should he eat rotten fish and meat. He should not eat food with bad colors, nor should he eat food with terrible smell. He should not eat food improperly cooked, nor should he eat food except at the proper time. He should not eat meat without being properly cut up, nor should he eat food except the proper sauce available.

Though there having plenty of meat at a feast, he should not eat more meat than rice.

Only drinking wine as he liked, yet he did not get drunk.

He should not eat dried meat and wine bought from a market.

Ginger must not be removed from the table after dinner, yet he should not eat it too much.

10.9

【原 文】

祭于公，不宿肉。祭肉不出三日。出三日，不食之矣。

【汉 译】

参加国君祭祀分得的祭肉，不能留着再过夜了。家里的祭肉，存放也不能超过三天。过了三天，就不吃了。

【英 译】

He didn't leave the sacrificial meat overnight allotted to him after participating in sacrificial rites held by his sovereign. The sacrificial meat at home was not allowed to be kept over three days, otherwise he would not eat it at all.

10.10

【原 文】

食不语，寝不言。

【汉　译】

吃饭的时候不说话，睡觉的时候不言语。

【英　译】

He did not converse with others while eating a meal, nor did he talk in bed.

10.11

【原　文】

虽疏食菜羹，必祭，必齐如也。

【汉　译】

即使吃粗饭、菜汤，临食前也要祭一祭，而且要恭恭敬敬。

【英　译】

Even if consuming the simple rice and vegetable soup, the Master was bound to take some from them before dinner as sacrificial offerings to the ancestors. Moreover, he did it deferentially during fast days.

10.12

【原　文】

席不正，不坐。

【汉　译】

坐席放得不正，不坐。

【英　译】

He did not sit on the mat which wasn't put properly.

10.13

【原　文】

乡人饮酒，杖者出，斯出矣。

【汉　译】

行过乡饮酒礼后，要等老年人都出去了，自己才能出去。

【英　译】

After drinking wine with his villagers in the country, the Master would certainly let the old people leave before him.

10.14

【原　文】

乡人傩，朝服而立于阼阶。

【汉　译】

逢乡人迎神驱鬼时，自己便穿上朝服，立在庙东边的台阶上。

【英　译】

When the villagers expelling the evil spirits and welcoming the deities, the Master wore his court robes and stood on the eastern step of ancestral temple.

10.15

【原　文】

问人于他邦，再拜而送之。

【汉　译】

孔子派使者向他国友人问候送礼，向使者拜两次给他再送行。

【英　译】

When asking a messenger to send regards or gifts to his friend in another state, the Master was bound to visit him twice and then see him off.

10.16

【原　文】

康子馈药，拜而受之。曰："丘未达，不敢尝。"

【汉　译】

季康子给孔子送药，孔子拜谢后接受了，说："我对这药性还不了解，不敢尝。"

【英　译】

After Ji Kangzi presented him some medicine, the Master expressed his gratitude before accepting it. However, he said, "As I do not know its properties, I dare not have a taste."

10.17

【原　文】

厩焚。子退朝，曰："伤人乎？"不问马。

【汉　译】

孔子家的马棚失火了，孔子退朝回来，问道："伤着人了吗？"却没有问到马。

【英　译】

The stable caught fire. On his returning from court, the Master asked, "Is anyone injured?" Nevertheless, he did not ask about his horses.

10.18

【原　文】

君赐食，必正席先尝之。君赐腥，必熟而荐之。君赐生，必畜之。侍食于君，君祭，先饭。

【汉　译】

国君赐给吃的，一定要摆正坐席先尝尝。国君赐给生肉，一定烧熟了先供奉祖宗。国君赐给活物，一定把它饲养起来。陪国君一起吃饭，在国君祭祀时，自己先吃饭。

【英　译】

When the lord gave him some food, the Master definitely put his mat properly and then had a taste. When the lord gave him some raw meat, he certainly had it cooked and then offered it as sacrifices to his ancestors. When the lord gave him a live animal, he invariably accepted and raised it. Accompanying the lord to have dinner, he definitely started off with the rice while his lord made an offering sacrifice.

10.19

【原　文】

疾，君视之，东首，加朝服，拖绅。

【汉　译】

孔子有病了，君主来探视他，他就面朝东躺着，身上盖着朝服，拖着大带子。

【英　译】

The Master was ill. The lord paid a visit for him. In the meantime, he was lying in bed with his head to the east, with his court robes covered his body and his big sash trailed on the ground.

10.20

【原　文】

君命召，不俟驾行矣。

【汉　译】

国君有事召见，孔子不等马车备好，就先步行走去了。

【英　译】

The lord called him in, and the Master would go on foot in advance without waiting for the horse and carriage at the ready.

10.21

【原　文】

入太庙，每事问。

【汉　译】

孔子进了太庙，对每件事情，他都要问一下。

【英　译】

The Master asked questions about everything after entering the temple offering sacrifices to the sovereign's ancestors.

10.22

【原　文】

朋友死，无所归，曰："于我殡。"

【汉　译】

朋友死了，没有人来办丧事，孔子说："丧事由我来办吧。"

【英　译】

A friend passed away, but nobody made the arrangements for his funeral affairs. The Master said, "I will be in charge of it."

10.23

【原　文】

朋友之馈，虽车马，非祭肉，不拜。

【汉　译】

朋友馈赠物品，除非是祭肉，即便是车马，孔子在接受时都不拜。

【英 译】

The Master only bowed to the sacrificial meat among the gifts given by his friends, not even including a carriage and the horses.

10.24

【原 文】

寝不尸，居不客。

【汉 译】

睡觉时，不要像死尸那样直挺着四肢。平时在家，也不必过分讲究容貌仪态像做客。

【英 译】

The Master did not lie like a stiff corpse while sleeping. Moreover, he did not care too much about his manners as a visitor while staying at home.

10.25

【原 文】

见齐衰者，虽狎，必变。见冕者与瞽者，虽亵，必以貌。

凶服者式之。式负版者。

有盛馔，必变色而作。

迅雷，风烈，必变。

【汉 译】

孔子见到穿丧服的，即使是平时很亲近的人，表情也必变得严肃起来，以示哀悼。见到戴礼帽的和盲人，即使是很熟悉的，也很有礼貌。

路遇穿丧服的人，便俯身伏在车前横木上，以示同情。看见背负国家图籍的人，同样俯身伏在车前横木上，以示敬意。

出席盛宴时，必变色起身致谢，表示恭敬。

遇到迅雷大风，也必变色，以示敬畏。

【英　译】

When meeting people in mourning dress, the Master definitely ass umed a solemn countenance even if they were very familiar to him. When meeting someone wearing a ceremonial hat or a blind man, he invariably showed deep respect for them even if they got well acquainted.

When meeting people wearing mourning apparel, he would lean a little bit forwards with his hands on the crossbar of his carriage to show sympathy; he would did the same towards a man carrying the official documents.

When attending a sumptuous banquet, he invariably took on a serious expression and stood up to express his gratitude.

When encountering a sudden clap of thunder and heavy wind, he also definitely assumed a solemn countenance to regard them with reverence.

10.26

【原　文】

升车，必正立，执绥。

车中，不内顾，不疾言，不亲指。

【汉　译】

上车时，必先端正地站好，手拉扶手带上车。

在车上，不回着头看，不高声说话，不用手指指画画。

【英　译】

While ascending a carriage, the Master invariably stood uprightly and grasped the handrail belt. When in the carriage, he neither looked backwards nor did he shout aloud or gesticulate here and there.

10.27

【原　文】

色斯举矣，翔而后集。曰："山梁雌雉，时哉时哉！"子路共之，三嗅而作。

【汉　译】

野鸡发现行人脸色不善就起身飞了，在空中盘旋一阵后才停在树上。孔子说："这些山梁上的雌野鸡，也懂得时宜呀！懂得时宜呀！"子路向它们拱拱手，野鸡长叫了几声飞走了。

【英　译】

Startled by people's unkind countenance, the pheasants rose up and started flying in the sky before alighting. The Master said, "The female pheasants on the hill, they also know what is appropriate to the occasion." Zi Lu bowed to the pheasants with his one hand cupped in the other, which sang aloud and then flew away.

先进篇第十一

11.1

【原　文】

子曰："先进于礼乐，野人也；后进于礼乐，君子也。如用之，则吾从先进。"

【汉　译】

孔子说："先学习礼乐而后做官的人，是没有爵位和俸禄的平民；先当了官而后再学习礼乐的，是原来就有爵位和俸禄的君子。倘若要我选用人才，我就选用先学习礼乐的人。"

【英　译】

The Master said, "It is generally acknowledged that a common people learnt etiquette and music first and then sought the official posts, whereas an aristocrat sought the official posts first and then learnt etiquette and music. If I had to select the talented people, I'd like to follow the former."

11.2

【原　文】

子曰："从我于陈、蔡者，皆不及门也。"

【汉　译】

孔子说："在陈、蔡饱受饥饿时跟随我的人，现在都不在我身边了。"

【英　译】

The Master said, "People are no longer learning knowledge at my home, who once experienced a lot of hardships and hunger with me in the states Chen and Cai."

11.3

【原　文】

德行：颜渊、闵子骞、冉伯牛、仲弓。言语：宰我、子贡。政事：冉有、季路。文学：子游、子夏。

【汉　译】

在孔子的弟子中，德行好的有颜渊、闵子骞、冉伯牛、仲弓。善于外交辞令的，有宰我、子贡。擅长政事的，有冉有、季路。通晓诗书礼乐等文献知识的，有子游、子夏。

【英　译】

Among the Master's disciples are those who have virtuous conduct: Yan Yuan, Min Ziqian, Ran Boniu and Zhong Gong; who are good at speech: Zai Wo and Zi Gong; who are skilled in government affairs: Ran You and Ji Lu; who are proficient at document culture and learning: Zi You and Zi Xia.

11.4

【原　文】

子曰："回也，非助我者也，于吾言无所不说。"

【汉　译】

孔子说："颜回呀，他不是对我有帮助的人，他对我讲的话没有不喜爱的。"

【英　译】

The Master said, "Yan Hui does not give me assistance, and yet he enjoys what I told him."

11.5

【原　文】

子曰："孝哉，闵子骞！人不间于其父母昆弟之言。"

【汉　译】

孔子说："闵子骞真孝呀！他的父母兄弟都夸他孝顺，别人听了，也从没有异议的。"

【英　译】

The Master said, "What a dutiful son Min Ziqian is! People heard his parents and brothers praise him, and yet none of them have any disagreements with them."

11.6

【原　文】

南容三复"白圭"，孔子以其兄之子妻之。

【汉　译】

南容反复朗诵诗经中关于白圭的诗句，告诫自己要说话谨慎，孔子就把自己的侄女嫁给了他。

【英　译】

Nan Rong recited over and over the verses of Odes concerning the white jade, and consequently the Master married his niece to him.

11.7

【原　文】

季康子问："弟子孰为好学？"孔子对曰："有颜回者好学，不幸短命死矣！今也则亡。"

【汉　译】

季康子问："你的弟子中谁最喜欢学习？"孔子回答说："有个

叫颜回的弟子好学，可惜他短命死了，现在没有像他那样的人了。"

【英　译】

Ji Kangzi asked the Master, "Who is eager to learn knowledge among your disciples?" The Master replied, "I have one disciple named Yan Hui who enjoys learning, but unfortunately he died very young. Now there is no one like him."

11.8

【原　文】

颜渊死，颜路请子之车以为之椁。子曰："才不才，亦各言其子也。鲤也死，有棺而无椁。吾不徒行以为之椁。以吾从大夫之后，不可徒行也。"

【汉　译】

颜渊死了，其父颜路请求孔子把车子卖掉给颜渊做一个椁。孔子说："不管有才能还是没才能，总归都是自己的儿子。我儿子鲤死时，也只有棺，没有椁，我并没有卖掉车子自己步行，来给他买椁。因为我以前曾做过大夫，不可以步行出门的。"

【英　译】

Yan Yuan died, and his father Yan Lu asked the Master to sell out his carriage to make an outer coffin for his son. The Master said, "No matter talented or not, they are all sons of their fathers. When Kong Li, my son died, I didn't sell out my carriage to provide him with an outer coffin because I was once a higher official named Daifu. It would have been improper for me to go out on foot, considering that I took my place after Daifu."

11.9

【原　文】

颜渊死，子曰："噫！天丧予！天丧予！"

【汉　译】

颜渊死了，孔子说："唉！是老天爷要我的命呀，是老天爷要我的命呀！"

【英　译】

When Yan Yuan died, the Master said, "Alas! Heaven has left me bereft! Heaven has bereft me! "

11.10

【原　文】

颜渊死，子哭之恸。从者曰："子恸矣！"曰："有恸乎？非夫人之为恸而谁为？"

【汉　译】

颜渊死了，孔子哭得很悲伤。跟随的人说："先生您太悲伤了！"孔子说："我是太悲伤了吗？我不为这个人悲伤，又为谁悲伤呢？"

【英　译】

When Yan Yuan died, the Master was weeping mournfully for him. His followers said, "How mournful you are!" The Master said, "Am I mournful? If I do not show undue sorrow for him, then for whom should I do?"

11.11

【原　文】

颜渊死，门人欲厚葬之。子曰："不可。"门人厚葬之。子曰："回也视予犹父也，予不得视犹子也。非我也，夫二三子也。"

【汉　译】

颜渊死了，孔子的学生们想要厚葬他，孔子说："不可以的。"学生们还是厚葬了颜渊。孔子说："颜回看待我就像父亲一样，而我却不能像儿子一般看待他。这可不是我的意思呀，都是那些学生们做的呀。"

【英　译】

When Yan Yuan died, the Master's disciples were to give him a sumptuous burial. Yet the Master said, "That won't do." However, they gave him a lavish burial. The Master said, "Yan Hui treated me as his father, yet I couldn't regard him as my son. This was not my own idea, and it was done by my disciples."

11.12

【原　文】

季路问事鬼神。子曰："未能事人，焉能事鬼？"曰："敢问死。"曰："未知生，焉知死？"

【汉　译】

子路问怎样侍奉鬼神，孔子说："活人还没有侍奉好，怎么能去侍奉鬼呢？"子路又问："敢问死是怎么回事？"孔子说："生的道理还没弄明白，怎么能知道死呢？"

【英　译】

Ji Lu asked how to serve the ghosts and the gods. The Master said, "You are unable to serve human beings faithfully. How can you serve the ghosts and spirits?"

Ji Lu asked again, "May I ask you about death?" The Master replied, "You have even no idea about life. How can you know anything about death?"

11.13

【原　文】

闵子侍侧，訚訚如也；子路，行行如也；冉有、子贡，侃侃如

143

也。子乐。"若由也，不得其死然。"

【汉　译】

闵子骞在孔子旁边侍奉，一派正直而恭敬的样子；子路是一派刚强的样子；冉有、子贡是一派温和快乐的样子。孔子很欢乐。但孔子又说："像仲由这样，怕难保天年呀！"

【英　译】

Serving the Master at his side, Min Ziqian seemed respectful and upright; Zi Lu appeared firm and unyielding; Ran You and Zi Gong looked gentle and cheerful. Consequently, the Master became joyous. Yet the Master said again, "I'm afraid, a man like Zhong You will not die of natural causes."

11.14

【原　文】

鲁人为长府。闵子骞曰："仍旧贯，如之何？何必改作？"子曰："夫人不言，言必有中。"

【汉　译】

鲁国人要改建长府。闵子骞说："照老样子不好吗？何必要改建呢？"孔子说："此人不说则已，一说话必然是中肯的。"

【英　译】

The people of the state Lu were to rebuild the national treasury. On hearing this, Min Ziqian said, "Why not retain its original look? Why must it be rebuilt?" The Master said, "This man seldom utters a word. Nevertheless, as long as he starts to talk, he is bound to hit the nail on the head."

11.15

【原　文】

子曰："由之瑟奚为于丘之门？"门人不敬子路。子曰："由也升堂矣，未入于室也。"

【汉　译】

孔子说："仲由呀，你为什么要在我这儿弹琴呢？"学生们听了，就瞧不起子路。孔子解释说："仲由在学问上已知大体，只是还不精深罢了。"

【英　译】

The Master said, "Zhong You! Why are you playing Se (a musical instrument like a zither) inside my door?" Therefore, the disciples didn't treat Zi Lu with respect. Then Confucius said, "You plays the music actually quite well, but he hasn't been proficient at it."

11.16

【原　文】

子贡问："师与商也孰贤？"子曰："师也过，商也不及。"曰："然则师愈与？"子曰："过犹不及。"

【汉　译】

子贡问："师和商二人，哪一个好些？"孔子说："师办事过头了，商办事又赶不上。"子贡说："那么是师好一些了？"孔子说："过头了和赶不上是一样的。"

【英　译】

Zi Gong asked, "Shi or Shang, who is better?" The Master said, "Shi often overdoes something, whereas Shang often fails to reach it." Zi Gong said, "Shi is better, then?" The Master said, "Going beyond is as bad as falling short."

11.17

【原　文】

季氏富于周公，而求也为之聚敛而附益之。子曰："非吾徒也。

小子鸣鼓而攻之，可也。"

【汉　译】

　　季氏的富有超过了周天子王朝的周公，而冉求还帮他搜刮而增加其财富。孔子说："冉求已不是我的弟子了，你们可以大张旗鼓地去声讨他。"

【英　译】

　　The Ji family is richer than the Duke of Zhou Dynasty，yet Ran Qiu still helped him to collect money and add his wealth. The Master said, "Ran Qiu is not my disciple. Therefore, you can beat the drum to attack him."

11.18

【原　文】

　　柴也愚，参也鲁，师也辟，由也喭。

【汉　译】

　　高柴愚直，曾参迟钝，颛孙师偏激，仲由鲁莽。

【英　译】

　　Gao Chai was stupid and straightforward. Zeng Can reacted slowly. Zhuan Sunshi took something to extremes. Zhong You acted rashly.

11.19

【原　文】

　　子曰："回也其庶乎？屡空。赐不受命，而货殖焉，臆则屡中。"

【汉　译】

　　孔子说："颜回的道德学问做得差不多了吧？可他常常陷于穷乏之中。端木赐没有经过官府准许去做买卖，但他猜行情竟常常猜中。"

【英　译】

The Master said, "Yan Hui is almost perfect, but he often lives in poverty. Duan Muci goes to do business without the governmental permission. Nevertheless, the truth of his conjecture is frequently confirmed with regard to the market situation"

11.20

【原　文】

子张问善人之道。子曰："不践迹，亦不入于室。"

【汉　译】

子张问何为善人。孔子说："善人若不踩着前人的脚印走，其学问和修养也难以到家。"

【英　译】

Zi Zhang asked about the way to become a good man. The Master said, "If he does not follow in other people's footsteps, a good man is unable to enter the inner room, i.e. the profound realm."

11.21

【原　文】

子曰："论笃是与，君子者乎？色庄者乎？"

【汉　译】

孔子说："听他说话诚恳，便赞许他，哪知他真是一位君子呢？还是仅仅外表庄重呢？"

【英　译】

The Master said, "You are going to pay someone a compliment if you just hear him say something with his honesty. Do you know whether he is a real gentleman or a hypocrite?"

11.22

【原　文】

　　子路问："闻斯行诸?"子曰："有父兄在,如之何其闻斯行之?"冉有问："闻斯行诸?"子曰："闻斯行之。"公西华曰："由也问'闻斯行诸',子曰'有父兄在',求也问'闻斯行诸',子曰'闻斯行之'。赤也惑,敢问。"子曰："求也退,故进之;由也兼人,故退之。"

【汉　译】

　　子路问："是不是听到了就该做呢?"孔子说："有父兄在上,怎么可以听到就做呢?"

　　冉有问："是不是听到了就该做呢?"孔子说："听到就可以做。"

　　公西华说："仲由问'是不是听到就该做',您说'有父兄在上';冉求问'是不是听到就该做',您说'听到就做'。我感到疑惑不解,敢再问个明白。"孔子说："冉求做事总是退缩,所以我要鼓励他上前;仲由一人兼做两人事,好勇过人,所以我要压压他。"

【英　译】

　　Zi Lu asked, "Go to do something immediately after hearing it?" The Master said, "As your father and elder brothers are still alive, how can you go and act immediately?" Ran You asked, "Go to do something immediately after hearing it?" The Master said, "Yes. That's right." Gong Xihua said, "Zhong You asked, 'Go to do something immediately after hearing it?' You said, 'As your father and elder brother are still alive, how can you go and act immediately?' Ran Qiu also asked, 'Go to do something immediately after hearing it?' But you said, 'Yes. That's right.' I feel very puzzled after hearing this. Would you please enlighten me?" The Master said, "As Ran Qiu always shrinks back, I have to encourage him. Nevertheless, as Zhong You is very bold, I have to hold him back."

11.23

【原　文】

　　子畏于匡,颜渊后。子曰："吾以女为死矣。"曰："子在,回何敢死？"

【汉　译】

孔子在匡地被围困，颜渊最后才逃出来。孔子说："我还以为你已经死了呢。"颜渊说："先生还活着，我哪敢轻易去死呢？"

【英　译】

When the Master was besieged in Kuang, Yan Yuan finally escaped from the place. The Master said, "I thought you must have been dead." Yan Yuan said, "How dare I die while you are still alive?"

11.24

【原　文】

季子然问："仲由、冉求可谓大臣与？"子曰："吾以子为异之问，曾由与求之问。所谓大臣者，以道事君，不可则止。今由与求也，可谓具臣矣。"曰："然则从之者与？"子曰："弑父与君，亦不从也。"

【汉　译】

季子然问："仲由和冉求能称得上大臣吗？"孔子说："我还以为你在问别的事，哪知你竟是问仲由和冉求两人呀。所谓大臣者，应该以仁道去侍奉君主，如果不合于道，宁肯辞职不干。现在仲由和冉求，只能算是备位充数的臣子罢了。"

季子然说："那么他们肯听话吗？"孔子说："若要杀父弑君，他们也是不会听从的。"

【英　译】

Ji Ziran asked, "Zhong You and Ran Qiu, can they be called the great ministers?" The Master said, "I had expected that you asked something else. It was beyond my expectancy that you asked about You and Qiu. As far as the great ministers are concerned, they should be those who serve their lord according to the Way and who will resign if not possible. Now men like You and Qiu can merely be considered two stop gap ministers."

Ji Ziran said, "Do they absolutely obey the orders as they are told?" The Master said, "If ordered to kill their fathers and the lord, they will certainly not do as a matter of fact."

11.25

【原　文】

子路使子羔为费宰。子曰："贼夫人之子。"子路曰："有民人焉，有社稷焉，何必读书，然后为学？"子曰："是故恶夫佞者。"

【汉　译】

子路让子羔去做费地的长官。孔子说："这是害了人家儿子。"

子路说："那里有百姓，有社稷，治理民事和祭祀神灵都是学习，为什么一定要读书才算学习呢？"

孔子说："所以我讨厌那利嘴善辩的人呀。"

【英　译】

Zi Lu asked Zi Gao to be the governor of Fei district. The Master said, "You're ruining the young man."

Zi Lu said, "There are the common people, god of land and god of grains. With regard to administration of the people and offering sacrifices to gods, all these are also considered learning. Why must only reading books be called learning?" The Master said, "It is for this reason that I hate the glib-tongued man."

11.26

【原　文】

子路、曾皙、冉有、公西华侍坐。

子曰："以吾一日长乎尔，毋吾以也。居则曰：'不吾知也！'如或知尔，则何以哉？"

子路率尔而对曰："千乘之国，摄乎大国之间，加之以师旅，因之以饥馑；由也为之，比及三年，可使有勇，且知方也。"

夫子哂之。

"求！尔何如？"

对曰："方六七十，如五六十，求也为之，比及三年，可使足民。如其礼乐，以俟君子。"

"赤！尔何如？"

对曰："非曰能之，愿学焉。宗庙之事，如会同，端章甫，愿为小相焉。"

"点！尔何如？"

鼓瑟希，铿尔，舍瑟而作，对曰："异乎三子者之撰。"

子曰："何伤乎？亦各言其志也。"

曰："莫春者，春服既成，冠者五六人，童子六七人，浴乎沂，风乎舞雩，咏而归。"

夫子喟然叹曰："吾与点也！"

三子者出，曾皙后。曾皙曰："夫三子者之言何如？"

子曰："亦各言其志也已矣。"

曰："夫子何哂由也？"

曰："为国以礼，其言不让，是故哂之。"

"唯求则非邦也与？"

"安见方六七十如五六十而非邦也者？"

"唯赤则非邦也与？"

"宗庙会同，非诸侯而何？赤也为之小，孰能为之大？"

【汉　译】

子路、曾皙、冉有、公西华四人陪孔子坐着。

孔子说："我是比你们年长几岁，不要因为我年长就不敢讲真话。你们平时常说没人了解自己，倘若有人了解你们，你们该怎么去做呢？"

了路急忙答道："倘使一个有千辆兵车的国家，夹在大国之间，外有强国军队入侵，国内又连年闹饥荒，让我去治理的话，只要三年，可使民众勇敢，且懂得礼义。"

孔子朝他微微一笑。

孔子又问："冉求，你怎么样？"

冉求答道："方圆六七十里或五六十里的小国，让我去治理的话，只要三年，就可使百姓衣食富足。至于礼乐教化，要等贤明君子来施行了。"

孔子又问："公西赤，你怎么样？"

公西赤答道："我不敢说自己能够做什么，只是愿意学习罢了。宗庙祭祀或诸侯会盟的时候，我愿穿着礼服，戴着礼帽，当一个赞礼的小相。"

孔子又问："曾点，你怎么样？"

曾晳在鼓瑟，瑟声稀落，铿地一声停下，放下瑟站起来，答道："我的想法和他们三位讲的不一样。"

孔子说："那有什么关系呢？只不过是各人谈谈自己的志向罢了。"

曾晳便说："暮春时节，穿上春天的夹衣，约上五六个成人，领着六七个童子，一起在沂水旁沐浴，到舞雩台上吹吹风，一路唱着歌回家。"

孔子喟然叹道："我赞同曾点的想法呀！"

子路、冉有、公西华三人退出了，曾晳留在后，他问孔子道："他们三位说的怎么样？"

孔子说："也就是各人谈谈自己的志向罢了。"

曾晳又问："那先生为什么笑仲由呢？"

孔子说："治国要讲礼义，可他说话一点也不谦虚，所以我笑他。"

曾晳又说："那冉求谈的不也是国家吗？"

孔子说："是呀，哪见方圆六七十里或五六十里的土地还算不上一个国家呢？"

曾晳又问："那公西赤谈的不也是治国吗？"

孔子说："宗庙祭祀和诸侯会盟，不是诸侯之事又是什么？公西赤如果只能当小司仪，那谁又能来当大司仪呢？"

【英　译】

Zi Lu, Zeng Xi, Ran You and Gong Xihua being seated in attendance, the Master said, "Do not mind that I am a little older than you. You usually say that you are not known and appreciated. Now, if your abilities being recognized, what would you be able to do?"

Zi Lu replied hurriedly, "I'd like to govern a state of a thousand chariots, which is situated between the big powers, invaded by the enemies, and harassed by the famines. Despite the fact, if I had the conduct of affairs in such a state, I could make the people courageous and know the rules of rites by the end of three years."

On hearing this, the Master just smiled at him.

The Master said to another disciple, "Ran Qiu, what about you?"

Ran Qiu then replied, "If I were to govern a state measured sixty or seventy li square, or even fifty or sixty li square, I would be able to make people well fed and dressed within three years. As for the rites and music, I would leave them to the good and wise men."

Then the Master turned to another disciple, and said, "Gong Xichi, what about you?"

Gong Xichi replied, "I'm afraid that I can do it well, but I'd like to learn. On ceremonial occasion of offering sacrifices at the ancestral temple and general assemblies of princes, I'd like to attend as a minor official in charge of ceremony, properly dressed in my formal hat and dress."

The Master said to the last of his four disciples, "And now, Zeng Dian, what about you?"

Strumming the last few notes on a sort of stringed instrument se, Zeng Dian stopped with a bang and then laid it aside, stood up and answered, "What I have in my mind is totally different from theirs."

The Master said, "What does it matter? It's just to express your own ideals."

Zeng Xi then said, "In late spring, I'd like to wear the spring dress, go with five or six adults and six or seven kids to bathe in the Yi river, then enjoy the gentle breeze on the Rain Altar, and at last go home singing all the way."

The Master said with a sigh, "Ah, I appreciate what Zeng Dian said."

Zeng Xi stayed behind after the three disciples left, and then he said, "What do you think of what my three fellow disciples said just now?"

The Master said, "They've just expressed their own ideals."

Zeng Xi said again, "Why did you smile at Zhong You?"

The Master said, "A state should be administered by the rules of rites. However, Zhong You was not modest, and therefore I smiled at him."

Zeng Xi asked again, "Did Ran Qiu say something concerning a state administration?"

The Master said, "As for governing a place measured sixty or seventy li square or indeed fifty or sixty *li* square, it deserves the name of a state administration, does not it?"

Zeng Xi asked again, "As to what Chi said, was he not concerned with a state administration?"

The Master said, "As regards offering sacrifices at the ancestral temple and general assemblies of princes, are they not big national issues? If Chi only acting as a minor official in the ceremony, who could be a high official?"

颜渊篇第十二

12.1

【原　文】

颜渊问仁。子曰："克己复礼为仁。一日克己复礼，天下归仁焉。为仁由己，而由人乎哉?"

颜渊曰："请问其目。"子曰："非礼勿视，非礼勿听，非礼勿言，非礼勿动。"

颜渊曰："回虽不敏，请事斯语矣。"

【汉　译】

颜渊问怎样做才是仁。孔子说："要克制和约束自己，使你的语言和行动都符合礼，这就是仁。一旦能做到了这点，天下就会归于仁道。行仁德全靠你自己，哪能靠别人呢?"

颜渊说："请问行仁德的具体要求。"孔子说："不合于礼的不看，不合于礼的不听，不合于礼的不说，不合于礼的不做。"

颜渊说："我虽然脑子迟钝，也要践行先生这番话。"

【英　译】

Yan Yuan asked about benevolence. The Master said, "Benevolence is conceived in giving oneself over to the observance of rites. As long as we observe this way, benevolence will be able to prevail in our society. Actually, the practice of benevolence totally depends on your own rather than on others."

Yan Yuan said, "I'd like to know the concrete way to practise benevolence." The Master said, "In regard to things going against the rites, you shouldn't look at them, nor listen to them, nor talk about them, nor engage in them."

Yan Yuan said, "Though I am not quick-witted, I'll still try my best to practise benevolence in accordance with your remarks."

12.2

【原　文】

仲弓问仁。子曰："出门如见大宾，使民如承大祭。已所不欲，勿施于人。在邦无怨，在家无怨。"仲弓曰："雍虽不敏，请事斯语矣。"

【汉　译】

仲弓问怎样做才是仁。孔子说："平常出门像去会见贵宾一样，役使百姓好像进行重大祭祀一般。自己所不喜欢的，就不要强加于别人。在诸侯国中做事无怨，为卿大夫做事也无怨。"仲弓说："我虽然脑子迟钝，也要照先生这番话去做。"

【英　译】

Zhong Gong asked about benevolence. The Master said, "When going out, you should behave respectfully as if you were meeting with the important guests. When employing the services of the common people, you should behave seriously as though you were holding the grand sacrificial rites. You should not impose on others what you yourself do not desire. In this way, you will not make any complaints either in a state or in a noble family."

Zhong Gong said, "Though I am not quick-witted, I'll still try my best to practise benevolence in accordance with your remarks."

12.3

【原　文】

司马牛问仁。子曰："仁者，其言也讱。"曰："其言也讱，斯谓之仁已乎？"子曰："为之难，言之得无讱乎？"

【汉　译】

司马牛问怎样做才是仁。孔子说："仁人说话很谨慎。"

司马牛说："说话谨慎，就叫仁吗？"孔子说："做起来已知很难，说起话来能不谨慎吗？"

【英　译】

Si Maniu asked about benevolence. The Master said, "The benevolent man often speaks cautiously." Si Maniu said, "Can a man be said to be benevolent just because he speaks cautiously?" The Master said, "When doing something is very difficult, how can it be advisable for us not to speak cautiously?"

12.4

【原　文】

司马牛问君子。子问："君子不忧不惧。"曰："不忧不惧，斯谓之君子已乎？"子曰："内省不疚，夫何忧何惧？"

【汉　译】

司马牛问怎样做才是君子。孔子说："君子不忧愁，也不恐惧。"

司马牛说："不忧愁，不恐惧，就是君子了吗？"

孔子说："自己内心自省，做到问心无愧，还有什么忧虑和恐惧呢？"

【英　译】

Si Maniu asked about gentleman. The Master said, "The gentleman neither worries about nor fears anything." Si Maniu said, "In that case, can a man be said to be a gentleman just because he does not worry about nor fears anything?" The Master said, "If he has self-examination upon his own, a man finds nothing to reproach himself on his conscience. Then, what worries and fears can he have?"

12.5

【原　文】

司马牛忧曰:"人皆有兄弟,我独亡。"子夏曰:"商闻之矣:'死生有命,富贵在天。'君子敬而无失,与人恭而有礼,四海之内,皆兄弟也。君子何患乎无兄弟也?"

【汉　译】

司马牛忧伤地说:"别人都有兄弟,唯独我没有。"子夏说:"我听说过:'死生都由命运主宰,富贵都由上天安排。'君子做事只要严肃认真,不出差错,对待别人恭敬有礼,那天下人就都是你的兄弟了。君子何必担心自己没有兄弟呢?"

【英　译】

Si Maniu said depressingly, "All men have brothers, but I have none." Zi Xia said, "I have heard it said, 'life and death are determined by your fate; wealth and honour depend on heaven.' As long as the gentleman works hard and makes no mistakes, is respectful of others and observant of the proprieties, he'll find that all men in the world are his brothers. What's the need for a gentleman to worry about not having any brothers?"

12.6

【原　文】

子张问明。子曰:"浸润之谮,肤受之愬,不行焉,可谓明也已矣。浸润之谮,肤受之愬,不行焉,可谓远也已矣。"

【汉　译】

子张问怎样才算明智。孔子说:"暗中传播的谗言和切肤之痛般的诬告,在你面前都行不通,那你就可以说是明智了。暗中传播的谗言,切肤之痛般的诬告,在你面前都行不通,那你就可以说是很有远见了。"

【英　译】

Zi Zhang asked about sensibility. The Master said, "When a man is not affected by the slanders on the sly or by the frames like knives cutting skin ruthlessly, he can be said to be sensible. Similarly, he can be said to be far-sighted."

12.7

【原　文】

子贡问政。子曰："足食，足兵，民信之矣。"子贡曰："必不得已而去，于斯三者何先？"曰："去兵。"子贡曰："必不得已而去，于斯二者何先？"曰："去食。自古皆有死，民无信不立。"

【汉　译】

子贡问如何处理政事。孔子说："要使粮食充足，军备充足，百姓信任政府。"子贡说："要是不得已，一定要去掉一项，那么在这三项中先去掉哪一项呢？"孔子说："先去掉军备。"子贡说："要是不得已，再去掉一项，那么在剩余的两项中先去掉哪一项呢？"孔子说："先去掉粮食。自古以来人皆有死，若百姓对政府失去信心，国家就不能存在了。"

【英　译】

Zi Gong asked about government affairs. The Master said, "You should give the common people enough grain, have the sufficient troops, and earn the people's trust." Zi Gong said, "If I have to give up one of these three, which one should be removed first?" The Master said, "Remove sufficient troops." Zi Gong said, "If I have to remove one of the remaining two, which one should be taken off first?" The Master said, "Give up abundant grain. It is acknowledged that death has been bound to happen to all the people since the ancient times. Nevertheless, the state will be unable to exist if without earning the people's trust."

12.8

【原　文】

棘子成曰："君子质而已矣，何以文为？"子贡曰："惜乎，夫子之说君子也！驷不及舌。文犹质也，质犹文也。虎豹之鞟犹犬羊之鞟。"

【汉　译】

棘子成说："君子只要本质好就够了，何必要那些礼仪之类的东西呢？"子贡说："遗憾呀，先生您居然这样谈论君子！真是'一言既出，驷马难追'呀！其实，本质和文采是同等重要的。犹如去了毛的虎豹皮和去了毛的犬羊皮，二者都是一样的。"

【英　译】

Ji Zicheng said, "Gentlemen should attach importance to their intrinsic qualities. What's the need to lay stress on the rites?" Zi Gong said, "I feel deeply regretful at your comments. Contrary to my expectations, you have talked about gentlemen like this. You know, words once spoken cannot be recalled. As a matter of fact, intrinsic qualities are like the rites, and vice versa. The pelt is cut of a tiger or a leopard, and its leather is no different from that of a dog or a sheep."

12.9

【原　文】

哀公问于有若曰："年饥，用不足，如之何？"有若对曰："盍彻乎？"曰："二，吾犹不足，如之何其彻也？"对曰："百姓足，君孰与不足？百姓不足，君孰与足？"

【汉　译】

鲁哀公问有若道："如遇年岁饥荒，国家用度不够，该怎么办呢？"

有若回答说："何不实行十成抽一的田税制呢？"哀公说："现在十成抽二，我都还不够用，怎么能十抽一呢？"

有若回答说:"假如百姓富足了,您怎么会不够用? 如果百姓贫穷了,您又怎么会够用呢?"

【英 译】

Duke Ai, the lord of the country Lu, asked You Ruo, "My country is suffering from financial difficulties due to the widespread famine. What should I do?" You Ruo replied, "Why don't you implement the state tax system, namely taxing the people one part in ten?" Duke Ai said, "It is not enough for me to meet the state expenditure in taxing the people two part in ten? Let alone taxing the people one part in ten." You Ruo said, "If the common people are wealthy, how are you unable to meet your expenditure? Similarly, if the ordinary people live in poverty, how are you able to meet your expenditure?"

12.10

【原 文】

子张问崇德、辨惑。子曰:"主忠信,徙义,崇德也。爱之欲其生,恶之欲其死。既欲其生,又欲其死,是惑也。'诚不以富,亦祗以异。'"

【汉 译】

子张问如何提高品德修养和辨别迷惑。孔子说:"以忠诚守信为主,唯义是从,这样就可以提高品德修养了。若喜欢一个人,就希望他长生不死;若对他讨厌,巴不得他立马死掉。既要他生,又要他死,这就是迷惑。这样做对自己实在没有好处,只是使人觉得怪异罢了。"

【英 译】

Zi Zhang asked about the exaltation of moral character and the resolution of perplexities. The Master said, "You should make it your predominant principle, i.e. to do your best for others, to keep trustworthy in what you say, and to let your thoughts conform to morality and justice. If you accomplish these, you will be able to exalt your moral character. As you love a man, you want him perpetually youthful; but as you loathe a man, you want him to die immediately. Your action is bound to incur the perplexities of life. Wish a man a long life and meanwhile hope he must die instantly. It is just like the meaning of the quotation from The Book of Songs, 'While it is not that you dislike the poor and love the rich, it is that you love the new and dislike the old.'"

12.11

【原　文】

齐景公问政于孔子。孔子对曰："君君，臣臣，父父，子子。"公曰："善哉！信如君不君，臣不臣，父不父，子不子，虽有粟，吾得而食诸？"

【汉　译】

齐景公向孔子询问治国之道，孔子答道："君主要像个君主，臣子要像个臣子，父亲要像个父亲，儿子要像个儿子。"景公说："妙极了！若君主不像个君主，臣子不像个臣子，父亲不像个父亲，儿子不像个儿子，尽管有粮食，我能吃得到吗？"

【英　译】

Duke Jing, the lord of the country Qi asked about government affairs. The Master said, "A monarch should be like a monarch. A minister should be like a minister. A father should be like a father. A son should be like a son." Duke Jing said, "That's great! If a monarch is not like a monarch, a minister is not like a minister, a father is not like a father, a son is not like a son, can I have anything to eat even if there is sufficient grain?"

12.12

【原　文】

子曰："片言可以折狱者，其由也与？"子路无宿诺。

【汉　译】

孔子说："仅凭一方言辞就可以断案的，大概只有仲由吧！"子路履行诺言，从不拖延。

【英　译】

The Master said, "If anyone can settle a lawsuit on the evidence of just one party, maybe it is only Zhong You who can do it." Zi Lu used to fulfill his promise and never put it off to the next day.

12.13

【原　文】

子曰："听讼，吾犹人也。必也使无讼乎？"

【汉　译】

孔子说："审理诉讼案件，我跟别人是一样的，重要的是使诉讼案件没有才好。"

【英　译】

The Master said, "In hearing lawsuit, mine is identical to the way of others. Nevertheless, it is essential for us to try to stop any lawsuit cases from happening!"

12.14

【原　文】

子张问政。子曰："居之无倦，行之以忠。"

【汉　译】

子张问从政之道。孔子说："在官位上不要懈怠，执行政令要出于忠心。"

【英　译】

Zi Zhang asked about administering government affairs. The Master said, "Tirelessly serve the people while being in the official position, and loyally implement the policies and decrees."

12.15

【原 文】

子曰:"博学于文,约之以礼,亦可以弗畔矣夫!"

【汉 译】

孔子说:"广泛学习文献知识,并且用礼来约束自己,就可以不背离君子之道了。"

【英 译】

The Master said, " Provided he studies the historical documents exte nsively and is restrained by the rites, a gentleman can avoid being out of the right way."

12.16

【原 文】

子曰:"君子成人之美,不成人之恶。小人反是。"

【汉 译】

孔子说:"君子成全别人的好事,而不促成别人的坏事。小人则恰恰相反。"

【英 译】

The Master said, " A gentleman aids others in doing a good deed, but he does not help them to do something evil. Nonetheless, a mean man has the contrary points."

12.17

【原 文】

季康子问政于孔子。孔子对曰:"政者,正也。子帅以正,孰敢不正?"

【汉　译】

季康子向孔子请教从政之道。孔子说："政就是正的意思。你自己带头走正道，谁还敢不走正道呢？"

【英　译】

Ji Kangzi asked about managing government affairs. The Master said, "Managing government affairs means being correct. As long as you take the lead in the right way, who dare not to follow you?"

12.18

【原　文】

季康子患盗，问于孔子。孔子对曰："苟子之不欲，虽赏之不窃。"

【汉　译】

季康子苦于盗贼猖獗，于是向孔子求教。孔子回答说："假若你自己不贪财，纵使你悬赏人去行窃，他们也是不会干的。"

【英　译】

Troubled by the thieves and robbers in the country, Ji Kangzi asked how to deal with them. The Master said, "If you yourself were not greedy for money, no one would commit theft even if a reward were offered for it."

12.19

【原　文】

季康子问政于孔子曰："如杀无道，以就有道，何如？"孔子对曰："子为政，焉用杀？子欲善而民善矣。君子之德风，小人之德草。草上之风，必偃。"

【汉　译】

季康子向孔子请教为政之道，他说："假若杀掉坏人来成全好人，怎么样？"孔子回答说："你治理政事，怎么要靠杀人呢？只要你心想行善，百姓自然也就向善了。居上位之人，其德行就像风，而百姓的德行就像草。风吹到草上，草必然会顺风倒下。"

【英　译】

Ji Kangzi asked the Master about managing government affairs, saying, "What would you think if, in order to help those who own the Way, I were to kill those who do not follow the Way?" The Master answered, "Why do you govern your country by killing people? So long as you yourself do the good deeds, the common people will become good. Actually, the gentlemen are like wind and the common people are like grass. Wind is blown over the grass which is bound to fall down."

12.20

【原　文】

子张问："士何如斯可谓之达矣？"子曰："何哉，尔所谓达者？"子张对曰："在邦必闻，在家必闻。"子曰："是闻也，非达也。夫达也者，质直而好义，察言而观色，虑以下人。在邦必达，在家必达。夫闻也者，色取仁而行违，居之不疑。在邦必闻，在家必闻。"

【汉　译】

子张问："读书人怎样做才算是'达'呢？"孔子说："你所说的'达'是什么意思？"子张说："'达'就是在诸侯国有名气，在卿大夫家中也有名声。"孔子说："这是名气，并不是'达'。所谓'达'，就是为人正直而讲信义，善于分析别人的言语，观察别人的脸色，总考虑居于人下。这种人在诸侯国一定显达，在卿大夫家也必然显达。至于有名气，就是表面上装得很有仁德，而行为却与此相反，常以仁人自居，而不加怀疑自己。这种人，在诸侯国一定有名气，在卿大夫家中也必定有名气。"

【英　译】

Zi Zhang asked, "How is an intellectual able to become 'illustrious and influential?'" The Master said, "What on earth do you mean by saying 'illustrious and influential?'" Zi Zhang said, "What I mean is an intellectual who is well known both in a state and in a noble family." The Master said, "That's the problem of 'well known,' but no 'illustrious and influential.' Now the term 'illustrious and influential' describes a man who is upright and faithful, sensitive to others' words, observant of their countenance, and always mindful of keeping modest. Such a kind of man is able to become 'illustrious and influential' both in a state and in a noble family. As regards the term 'well known', it describes a man who superficially pretends to be benevolent and claims to be benevolent on his own. Such a man is sure to be well known whether he serves in a state or in a noble family."

12.21

【原　文】

樊迟从游于舞雩之下，曰：“敢问崇德，修慝，辨惑。”子曰：“善哉问！先事后得，非崇德与？攻其恶，无攻人之恶，非修慝与？一朝之忿，忘其身，以及其亲，非惑与？”

【汉　译】

樊迟陪孔子出游于舞雩台下，说道：“请问怎样才能提高品德修养，改正内心的过错，明辨是非呢？”孔子说：“问得好啊！把事情先做好，把名利放在后面，不就是提高品德修养了吗？先检查自己的过失，而不去指责别人的过失，不就是改正了过错吗？忍不住一时的气愤，便忘了自身的安危，甚至连累到了自己的亲人，这不是糊涂吗？”

【英　译】

Attending the sacrificial altar for rain with the Master, Fan Chi said, "May I ask you any questions about an improvement of virtue, correction of mistakes, and resolution of perplexities?" The Master said, "What an excellent question! Bearing hard ship first and then seeking fame and wealth, is it not an improvement of virtue? Doing self-criticism but not criticizing others, is it not for one to correct mistakes? A sudden fit of anger making you forget your own safety, or even that of your close relatives, is that not being perplexed?"

12.22

【原　文】

　　樊迟问仁。子曰："爱人。"问知。子曰："知人。樊迟未达。子曰："举直错诸枉，能使枉者直。"樊迟退，见子夏曰："乡也吾见于夫子而问知，子曰'举直错诸枉，能使枉者直'，何谓也?"子夏曰："富哉言乎！舜有天下，选于众，举皋陶，不仁者远矣。汤有天下，选于众，举伊尹，不仁者远矣。"

【汉　译】

　　樊迟问什么是仁。孔子说："爱人。"樊迟又问什么是智，孔子说："善于识别人。"

　　樊迟想不通。孔子说："选拔正直的人，把他们放在邪恶的人的位置之上，能使邪恶的人正直起来。"

　　樊迟退了出来，见到子夏说："我刚才见到老师，问他什么是智,老师说'选拔正直的人，把他们放在邪恶的人的位置之上，能使邪恶的人正直起来'，这是什么意思?"

　　子夏说："这话含义多么深刻呀！舜有了天下后，在众人中挑选皋陶来任用，那些不仁的人就远去了。汤有了天下后，在众人中挑选伊尹来举用，那些不仁的人也远去了。"

【英　译】

Fan Chi asked about benevolence. The Master said, "Love your people." Then he asked about wisdom. The Master said, "Know your people." Fan Chi didn't grasp his meaning. The Master said, "Raise the upright men and set them over position of the evils. This can make the evils upright." Fan Chi came out and saw Zi Xia, saying, "A moment ago, I went to see the Master and asked him about wisdom. The Master said, 'Raise the upright men and set them over position of the evils. This can make the evils upright.' What did he convey us in his words?" Zi Xia said, "What extremely profound words! When Shun possessed the state, he raised Gao Yan from the multitude and consequently those who were not benevolent were at a great distance. When Tang possessed the state, he raised Yi Yin from the multitude and consequently those who were not benevolent were at a great distance."

12.23

【原　文】

子贡问友。子曰："忠告而善道之，不可则止，毋自辱焉。"

【汉　译】

子贡问交友之道。孔子说："要忠言劝告他，好好引导他，如果不听也就罢了，不要自取其辱。"

【英　译】

Zi Gong asked about the way to treat friends. The Master said, "You should give sincere advice and appropriate guidance for your friend. However, if he does not accept your advice, you'd better just leave it at that and won't get self-inflicted insult for yourself."

12.24

【原　文】

曾子曰："君子以文会友，以友辅仁。"

【汉　译】

曾子说："君子以文章学问来交朋友，靠朋友帮助来培养仁德。"

【英　译】

Zeng Zi said, "A gentleman makes friends through his writings and learning, but improves benevolence with the help of his friends."

子路篇第十三

13.1

【原　文】

　　子路问政。子曰："先之劳之。"请益。曰："无倦。"

【汉　译】

　　子路问从政之道。孔子说："给百姓带好头，再让他们辛勤劳作。"子路请求多讲一些。孔子说："按上面的要求行事，不可懈怠。"

【英　译】

　　Zi Lu asked about the way of administering government affairs. The Master said, "You should set an example yourself before encouraging the common people to work hard." Then Zi Lu asked his master to say more. The Master said, "You should obey an order of your superior and never slack off."

13.2

【原　文】

　　仲弓为季氏宰，问政。子曰："先有司，赦小过，举贤才。"曰："焉知贤才而举之?"子曰："举尔所知；尔所不知，人其舍诸?"

【汉　译】

　　仲弓做了季氏家的总管，问老师如何管理政事。孔子说："教导下属各负其责，宽容他们的小过错，选拔优秀人才。"

　　仲弓说："如何知道谁是贤才而提拔他们呢?"孔子说："选拔你

自己所了解的，那些你不熟悉的，难道别人会埋没他们吗？"

【英　译】

As a steward of the Ji family, Zhong Gong asked about administering government affairs. The Master said, "Let your subordinates take charge of their own jobs, try to bear their minor faults and promote the talents among them." Zhong Gong asked, "How do I recognize those who are the real talents and promote them?" The Master said, "Promote those you know very well. As for those you don't know, do you think that they will be stifled?"

13.3

【原　文】

子路曰："卫君待子而为政，子将奚先？"子曰："必也正名乎！"子路曰："有是哉，子之迂也！奚其正？"子曰："野哉，由也！君子于其所不知，盖阙如也。名不正，则言不顺；言不顺，则事不成；事不成，则礼乐不兴；礼乐不兴，则刑罚不中；刑罚不中，则民无所措手足。故君子名之必可言也，言之必可行也。君子于其言，无所苟而已矣。"

【汉　译】

子路说："若卫君等着先生去主政，您打算从何处着手？"孔子说："首先要正名分呀！"子路说："您真是太迂腐了！为什么要去正名呢？"孔子说："仲由呀，你太粗野了！君子对于自己不知道的事，应该采取存疑的态度。如果名分不正，说话就不顺当；说话不顺当，事情就难办成；事情办不成，也就不能兴礼乐；礼乐制度不兴盛，刑罚就不会得当；刑罚不得当，老百姓便会手足无措，不知如何是好。所以君子定下名，一定要能说得出口，说出来了一定要可行。君子对于自己说出的话，不能有一点马虎罢了。"

【英　译】

Zi Lu asked, "If the Lord of Wei left administration of his state in your charge, what would you set about?" The Master said, "I'd like to start with the rectification of names." Zi Lu said, "Is it so? You're too pedantic, I suppose. What's the use to set about rectification of names?" The Master said, "Zhong You, how vulgar you are! As regards something unknown, a gentleman is expected to reserve his suspicion in mind. If names are not rectified, what you said will sound unreasonable. If your words sound unreasonable, you'll accomplish nothing. If nothing is accomplished, rites and music will not thrive. If rites and music do not flourish, penalty will not be exactly fair. If penalty is unfair, the common people will be at loss for what to do next. Therefore, if a gentleman names something, the name is sure to be called, and if he says something, it is bound to be practicable. As to what he said, the gentleman is never careless."

13.4

【原　文】

　　樊迟请学稼。子曰："吾不如老农。"请学为圃。曰："吾不如老圃。"樊迟出，子曰："小人哉，樊须也！上好礼，则民莫敢不敬；上好义，则民莫敢不服；上好信，则民莫敢不用情。夫如是，则四方之民襁负其子而至矣，焉用稼？"

【汉　译】

　　樊迟向孔子请教学种庄稼。孔子说："我不如老农。"樊迟又请教如何种蔬菜。孔子说："我不如老菜农。"樊迟退出去后，孔子说："樊迟真是个乡野小人啊！当权者只要能讲求礼仪，老百姓就不敢不敬；当权者只要能讲求道义，老百姓就不敢不服；当权者只要能讲求信用，百姓就不敢不以真情对待。能做到这样，四方百姓都会背着他们的小孩来投奔你，何必自己学种庄稼呢？"

【英　译】

　　Fan Chi asked his Master how to grow crops. The Master said, "I'm not as good as an old farmer." Then he asked how to grow vegetables. The Master said, "I'm not as good as an old gardener." After Fan Chi left, the Master said, "What a short-sighted man Fan Xu is! So long as the leaders observe the rites, none of the common people will dare not to stand in awe of them. So long as the leaders initiate justice, none of the common people will dare not to follow you. So long as the leaders keep their words, none of the common people will dare not to treat them wholeheartedly. If so, the common people from afar and wide will come to you with their little children strapped on their backs. What's the need for you to grow crops?"

13.5

【原　文】

子曰："诵诗三百，授之以政，不达；使于四方，不能专对。虽多，亦奚以为?"

【汉　译】

孔子说："熟读《诗经》三百篇，让他处理政事，却不能通达；派他出使外国，却不能独立应对。读书虽多，又有何用?"

【英　译】

The Master said, "If he is asked to manage government affairs, a man cannot do it; if he is sent to foreign states, a man can not accomplish the task alone. As for such a man, what's the use for him to skillfully recite the 300 poems of *The Book of Odes*?"

13.6

【原　文】

子曰："其身正，不令而行；其身不正，虽令不从。"

【汉　译】

孔子说："当权者本身品行端正，即使不下命令，百姓也会执行；当权者本身行为不正，即使下命令，百姓也不会服从。"

【英　译】

The Master said, "As long as the leaders behave very well in public, the common people will obey them without orders being issued. Otherwise, if the leaders do not behave well, the common people won't obey them even if orders are given."

13.7

【原　文】

子曰："鲁卫之政，兄弟也。"

【汉　译】

孔子说："鲁国和卫国的政事，就像兄弟一样啊!"

【英　译】

The Master said, "As regards the government affairs between the two states of Lu and Wei, they are just like those between brothers."

13.8

【原　文】

子谓卫公子荆："善居室。始有，曰：'苟合矣。'少有，曰：'苟完矣。'富有，曰：'苟美矣。'"

【汉　译】

孔子谈及卫国大夫公子荆时说："他善于居家理财，会过日子。刚开始有一点时，他就说：'凑合着就够了。'稍微多一些时，他便说：'将就着就完备了。'当家财更多时，他就说：'差不多算是完美了。'"

【英　译】

Talking about Prince Jing of the state Wei, the Master said, "He's adept in the way of managing family money matters. When there is a little money at the beginning, he would say, 'That's enough. Just make do with it.' When there is a little bit more money, he would say, 'It is almost complete and adequate.' When there is much money, he would say, 'It's nearly called perfect.'"

13.9

【原　文】

　　子适卫，冉有仆。子曰："庶矣哉！"冉有曰："既庶矣，又何加焉？"曰："富之。"曰："既富矣，又何加焉？"曰："教之。"

【汉　译】

　　孔子去卫国，冉有给他驾车。孔子说："这里人真多啊！"冉有说："人口多了以后，又该做些什么呢？"孔子说："让他们富裕起来。"冉有又说："富裕以后，又该做些什么呢？"孔子说："对他们进行教化。"

【英　译】

　　When the Master went to the state Wei, Ran You drove the cart for him. The Master said " There are large numbers of people in the state Wei." Ran You said, "After the state has adequate people, what else has to be done?" The Master said, "Make them wealthy." Ran You said, "What else has to be done after their becoming rich?" The Master said. "They should be educated and persuaded."

13.10

【原　文】

　　子曰："苟有用我者，期月而已可也，三年有成。"

【汉　译】

　　孔子说："假如有人用我来治理国家，一年时间就会有起色，三年后会很有成效。"

【英　译】

　　The Master said, "If I am employed in charge of a state administration, initial success will be achieved in just one year, and great achievements will undoubtedly be made three years later."

13.11

【原　文】

　　子曰："'善人为邦百年，亦可以胜残去杀矣。'诚哉是言也！"

【汉　译】

　　孔子说："'善人治理国家一百年，也可以消除残暴、废除杀戮。'这句话说得正确呀！"

【英　译】

　　The Master said, "'If good men govern a country for a hundred years, brutality will be surmounted and wonton killing of innocent people will also be avoided.' What splendid remarks!"

13.12

【原　文】

　　子曰："如有王者，必世而后仁。"

【汉　译】

　　孔子说："如有一位王者兴起，也一定要三十年的时间，才能实行仁政。"

【英　译】

　　The Master said, "If a true king appears, it is bound to take thirty years for him to realize administration by policy of benevolence."

13.13

【原　文】

　　子曰："苟正其身矣，于从政乎何有？不能正其身，如正人何？"

【汉　译】

孔子说："假如使自身品行端正了，处理政事还会有什么困难呢？若自身品行不端正，又怎能使别人端正呢？"

【英　译】

The Master said, "If a man manages to behave well, what difficulties will there be for him to take office? If he cannot behave well, how can he ask others to set right his behavior?"

13.14

【原　文】

冉子退朝。子曰："何晏也？"对曰："有政。"子曰："其事也。如有政，虽不吾以，吾其与闻之。"

【汉　译】

冉有退朝回来，孔子问："这么晚才回来呀？"冉有回答说："有政务商讨。"孔子说："怕是私事吧？如有政务，虽然不用我，我也会知道的。"

【英　译】

Ran Zi returned from the court. The Master said, "Why do you come back so late?" Ran Zi said, "We have some government affairs to deal with." The Master said, "They might have been the personal affairs, I suppose. If there are the government affairs, I'll know them even if I am no longer employed."

13.15

【原　文】

定公问："一言而可以兴邦，有诸？"孔子对曰："言不可以若是其几也。人之言曰：'为君难，为臣不易。'如知为君之难也，不几乎一言而兴邦乎？"

曰："一言而丧邦，有诸?"

孔子对曰："言不可以若是其几也。人之言曰：'予无乐乎为君，唯其言而莫予违也。'如其善而莫之违也，不亦善乎? 如不善而莫之违也，不几乎一言而丧邦乎?"

【汉　译】

鲁定公问："一句话可以使国家兴盛，有这样的事吗?"

孔子回答说："话不可以这么说，但意思差不多的话是有的。有人说：'做君主难，做臣子不易。'若知道做君主难，就会认真去做，不就近乎一句话可以使国家兴盛吗?"

定公又问："一句话可以亡国，有这样的事吗?"

孔子回答说："话不可以这么说，但意思差不多的话是有的。有人说：'我做国君没感受到什么快乐，唯一感到快乐的是我说话没有人敢违抗我。'若话说得对而没有人违抗，不也是很好吗? 若话说得不对而没有人敢违抗，这不近乎一句话可以亡国吗?"

【英　译】

Duke Ding asked, "Is there such a single saying that can make a state prosperous?"

The Master said, "A single saying cannot do that quite well, yet there are similar words. People say, 'It's difficult to be a lord, and it's not easy to be a courtier either.' If the lord knows the difficulty of being a lord, isn't it similar to one single word that can make a country flourishing? Are there any words like this?"

Duke Ding said, "Is there such a saying that can ruin a state?"

The Master said, "A single saying cannot do that quite well. There is a saying, 'I do not enjoy being a lord, apart from the point that no one dare to go against what I say.' If what he says is correct and no one resists him, that's good. Nonetheless, if what he says is wrong and no one resists him, isn't it similar to a case of one single word that can ruin a country?"

13.16

【原　文】

叶公问政。子曰："近者说，远者来。"

【汉　译】

叶公问为政之道，孔子说："离您近的人感到高兴，离您远的人前来归附您。"

【英　译】

Duke She asked about administration of government affairs. The Master said, "Make the people nearby delightful and make the people far away come to follow you."

13.17

【原　文】

子夏为莒父宰，问政。子曰："无欲速，无见小利。欲速，则不达；见小利，则大事不成。"

【汉　译】

子夏做了莒父的长官，他向孔子询问为政之道。孔子说："不要图快，不要贪小利。求快反而达不到目的；贪小利就成不了大事。"

【英　译】

After becoming a prefect of Ju Fu, Zi Xia asked about administration of government affairs. The Master said, "Don't be in a hurry to do something. Don't be greedy for just petty gains. Otherwise, the main purpose will not be achieved and the great task will not be accomplished."

13.18

【原　文】

叶公语孔子曰："吾党有直躬者，其父攘羊，而子证之。"孔子曰："吾党之直者异于是：父为子隐，子为父隐。——直在其中矣。"

【汉　译】

叶公告诉孔子说："我们那里有个正直的人，他父亲偷了别人的羊，他便告发了父亲。"孔子说："我们那里正直的人与你们那儿的不一样：父亲为儿子隐瞒，儿子为父亲隐瞒。——正直就表现在这里了。"

【英　译】

Duke She said to the Master, "There is an upright man in my hometown. He exposed his father who had stolen a sheep." The Master said, "The upright people in my hometown are quite different from those who are straight in yours. Fathers conceal their sons' mistakes and vice versa. As a matter of fact, straightness is to be found in such behaviour."

13.19

【原　文】

樊迟问仁。子曰："居处恭，执事敬，与人忠。虽之夷狄，不可弃也。"

【汉　译】

樊迟问怎样可以称为仁。孔子说："平日闲居时态度谦恭，做起事来认真谨慎，待人要诚恳。即使到夷狄少数民族地区，也不可背弃这些品质。"

【英　译】

Fan Chi asked about benevolence. The Master said, "Behave yourself properly at home, do things carefully outside, and treat people wholeheartedly. You shouldn't disregard the qualities even if you go to live among the barbarians."

13.20

【原　文】

子贡问曰："何如斯可谓之士矣？"子曰："行己有耻，使于四方，不辱君命，可谓士矣。"曰："敢问其次。"曰："宗族称孝焉，乡党称弟焉。"曰："敢问其次。"曰："言必信，行必果，硁硁然小人哉！抑亦可以为次矣。"曰："今之从政者何如？"子曰："噫！斗筲之人，何足算也？"

【汉　译】

　　子贡问："怎样才可以算士呢？"孔子说："自己的行为有知耻之心，出使外国能完成君主使命，就可以称作士了。"子贡又问："请问次一等的呢？"孔子说："宗族人称赞他孝顺父母，同乡人称赞他尊敬兄长。"子贡又说："敢问再次一等的呢？"孔子说："说话讲信用，做事很果断，像石头般坚硬固执，那是小人呀！但也可以算是再次一等的士了。"子贡问："现在那些当官的怎么样？"孔子说："唉！这些气量狭小之人，何足挂齿！"

【英　译】

　　Zi Gong asked, "How can a man become a Gentleman?" The Master said, "A man should have a sense of shame in the way he conducts himself and he should accomplish his mission when sent abroad. Such a man can be said to be a Gentleman." Zi Gong asked, "How about an inferior one?" The Master said, "A man is praised for showing filial respect to his parents in the clan and for respecting for the elderly in his hometown." Zi Gong asked, "How about an inferior one again?" The Master said, "A man can put his words into deeds and he can see his actions through to the end. Though he shows a stubborn petty-mindedness, such a man is qualified to the Gentleman of the last rank." Zi Gong asked, "How about the officials in the present day?" The Master said, "Oh, they are of such narrow-minded people who are not worth mentioning."

13.21

【原　文】

　　子曰："不得中行而与之，必也狂狷乎！狂者进取，狷者有所不为也。"

【汉　译】

　　孔子说："找不到言行合乎中庸之道的人与之交往，必定会结交狂狷之人了。狂者行为激进，勇于进取；狷者做事有所保留，不肯积极主动地去做。"

【英　译】

The Master said, "I cannot find and associate with the men whose words and deeds conform to the doctrine of golden mean. Therefore, I have to associate with the frantic men and the reserved men. For that reason, the frantic men dare to do things, but the reserved men often shrink back."

13.22

【原　文】

子曰："南人有言曰：'人而无恒，不可以作巫医。'善夫！'不恒其德，或承之羞。'"子曰："不占而已矣。"

【汉　译】

孔子说："南方人有句话说：'人若没有恒心，不可以做巫医。'这话说得好呀！《易经》上说：'不能始终如一地坚守自己的德操，就会招致羞辱。'"孔子说："这样的人不去占卦就罢了。"

【英　译】

The Master said, "The southerners in China have a common saying, 'A man devoid of perseverance can not be a witch doctor.' What a wonderful remark! There's also a saying in *Yi Books*, 'If he is unable to keep standards of virtue, a man will be subjected to humiliation.'" Then the Master said, "It's nothing. Such a sort of man doesn't want to divine by means of Eight Diagrams."

13.23

【原　文】

子曰："君子和而不同，小人同而不和。"

【汉　译】

孔子说："君子能和谐相处，但不盲从附和；小人一味附和，却不能和谐共处。"

【英　译】

The Master said, "The gentleman lives constantly in harmony with others but doesn't echo with them. However, the mean man always chimes in with others to say the right things and actually he usually does exactly the opposite."

13.24

【原　文】

子贡问曰："乡人皆好之，何如？"子曰："未可也。"

"乡人皆恶之，何如？"子曰："未可也。不如乡人之善者好之，其不善者恶之。"

【汉　译】

子贡问孔子道："全乡村人都喜欢的人，这人怎么样？"孔子回答道："还不行。"

子贡又问道："全乡村人都讨厌的人，您觉得怎么样？"孔子回答道："还不行。不如全乡村的好人都喜欢他，全乡村的坏人都憎恨他。"

【英　译】

Zi Gong asked, "As for a man, if all the people in the town like him, what do you think of the man?" The Master said, "It's hard to say." Then Zi Gong asked, "As far as a man is concerned, if all the people in the town detest him, what do you think of him?"

The Master said, "It's hard to say. It would be better if all the good people in the town like him and meanwhile all the bad people in the town dislike him."

13.25

【原　文】

子曰："君子易事而难说也。说之不以道，不说也；及其使人也，器之。小人难事而易说也。说之虽不以道，说也；及其使人也，求备焉。"

【汉　译】

孔子说："在君子手下做事容易，要讨他的喜欢却很难。不用正当方式去讨他喜欢，他会不高兴的；但等到他用人时，他却会量才使用。在小人手下做事很难，而讨他喜欢却容易。即使用不正当的方式去讨好他，他也会高兴的；可等到他用人时，他会百般挑剔，求全责备。"

【英　译】

The Master said, "It's easy to serve a gentleman but it's difficult to please him. The gentleman will not be happy if you do not follow the Way to please him, but when it comes to employ others, he will do so according to their abilities. Nevertheless, it's difficult to serve a mean man but it's easy to please him. The mean man will be happy even if you do not follow the Way to please him, but when it comes to employ others, he demands perfection for them."

13.26

【原　文】

子曰："君子泰而不骄，小人骄而不泰。"

【汉　译】

孔子说："君子安宁而不骄傲，小人骄傲而不安宁。"

【英　译】

The Master said, "A gentleman feels at ease but not arrogant, yet the mean man feels arrogant but not calm."

13.27

【原　文】

子曰："刚、毅、木、讷近仁。"

【汉　译】

孔子说："刚强、坚毅、朴实、言语谨慎，这些品德近于仁。"

【英　译】

The Master said, "There are four good qualities such as resoluteness, unyielding, simplicity and cautious in speech, which are close to benevolence ."

13.28

【原　文】

子路问曰："何如斯可谓之士矣？"子曰："切切偲偲，怡怡如也，可谓士矣。朋友切切偲偲，兄弟怡怡。"

【汉　译】

子路问道："怎样做才可称为士呢？"孔子说："互相督促批评，又能和睦相处，就可称作士了。朋友之间是互相勉励，兄弟之间是和睦相处。"

【英　译】

Zi Lu asked, "How does a man deserve to be called a Gentleman?" The Master said, "One is called a Gentleman who offers constructive criticism for others and keeps a friendship with them. Earnestly encourage each other among friends and keep genial among brothers."

13.29

【原　文】

子曰："善人教民七年，亦可以即戎矣。"

【汉　译】

孔子说："善人在位，教导民众七年时间，也可以让他们上战场了。"

【英　译】

The Master said, "After a good man became a ruler, the common people have been trained for seven years and then they should be ready to take up arms."

13.30

【原　文】

子曰："以不教民战，是谓弃之。"

【汉　译】

孔子说："若没有经过教导训练，就让民众去打战，可以说是让他们去送命。"

【英　译】

The Master said, "The common people are sent to war without being trained, and it means to abandon them."

宪问篇第十四

14.1

【原　文】

宪问耻。子曰："邦有道，谷；邦无道，谷，耻也。"

"克、伐、怨、欲不行焉，可以为仁矣？"子曰："可以为难矣，仁则吾不知也。"

【汉　译】

原宪问什么是耻辱。孔子说："国家政治清明，做官领俸禄；国家政治黑暗，也去做官领俸禄，这就是耻辱。"

原宪又问道："好胜、自夸、怨恨和贪婪这四样毛病都没有，可以算得上仁吗？"孔子说："可以算得上难能可贵，至于是否是仁，那我就不知道了。"

【英　译】

Yuan Xian asked about what constituted dishonor. The Master said, "When there is justice and order prevailing in the country, you can hold an official post. When there is no justice and order across the country, you are still eager to seek an official post. Such an action is dishonorable."

Yuan Xian asked again, "If a man has no ambition and vanity and envy and greedy, may he be considered to be benevolent?" The Master said, "It may be considered as something difficult to achieve, but I don't know that it constitutes benevolence."

14.2

【原　文】

子曰："士而怀居，不足以为士矣。"

【汉　译】

孔子说："读书人若留恋其安逸的家庭生活，就不配称作读书人。"

【英　译】

The Master said, "If a gentleman is unwilling to leave his comfortable home, he can not be considered to a true gentleman."

14.3

【原　文】

子曰："邦有道，危言危行；邦无道，危行言孙。"

【汉　译】

孔子说："国家政治清明，言语要正直，行为也要正直；国家政治黑暗，行为仍要正直，但言语要谦和。"

【英　译】

The Master said, "When there is justice and order prevailing in the country, a man should be fair-minded in his speech and action. When there is no justice and order across the country, a man should be fair-minded in his action but be amiable in his speech."

14.4

【原　文】

子曰："有德者必有言，有言者不必有德。仁者必有勇，勇者不必有仁。"

【汉　译】

孔子说："有仁德者一定会有好言语，可有好言语者未必就有仁德。仁人必定有勇气，但有勇之人未必有仁德。"

【英 译】

The Master said, "A man of humanity is sure to make memorable remarks, yet a man who makes memorable remarks is not necessarily endowed with humanity. A humane man certainly has great courage, but a courageous man does not naturally possess courage."

14.5

【原 文】

南宫适问于孔子曰:"羿善射,奡荡舟,俱不得其死然。禹、稷躬稼而有天下。"夫子不答。南宫适出,子曰:"君子哉若人!尚德哉若人!"

【汉 译】

南宫适对孔子说:"羿擅长射箭,奡能陆地行舟,但他们都不得好死。禹和稷亲自下田种庄稼,他们却得了天下。"孔子对此没有回答。南宫适退出去后,孔子说:"这人可是个君子呀!这人真是个崇尚道德的人呀!"

【英 译】

Nan Gongkuo asked the Master, "Yi was a renowned man in ancient time who was skilled in archery, and Ao was another famous man who was strong enough to push a boat over the land; yet both of them finally came to an unnatural death. There were also two famous men named Yu and Ji in ancient time, who tilled in the fields and planted the crops; however, both of them eventually gained the Empire." The Master made no reply at that time. After Nan Gongkuo left, the Master said, "How really wise and honorable that man is! How much he values morality for sure!"

14.6

【原 文】

子曰:"君子而不仁者有矣夫,未有小人而仁者也。"

【汉 译】

孔子说："君子之中可能有不仁义的人，小人中不会有仁义之人。"

【英 译】

The Master said, "There may be some men without having humanity among the gentlemen, yet there is certainly no humanitarian amongst the mean men."

14.7

【原 文】

子曰："爱之，能勿劳乎？忠焉，能勿诲乎？"

【汉 译】

孔子说："爱他，能不让他劳苦吗？忠于他，能不教诲他吗？"

【英 译】

The Master said, "Even if you love anyone, can't you make him work hard? Even though you are faithful to anyone, can't you give him instruction?"

14.8

【原 文】

子曰："为命，裨谌草创之，世叔讨论之，行人子羽修饰之，东里子产润色之。"

【汉 译】

孔子说："郑国制定外交政策法令，由裨谌来起草，世叔提意见，外交官子羽进行修改，最后东里子产在文字上加以润色。"

【英 译】

The Master said, "In the formulation of foreign policies and documents, one minister Bi Chen made the first draft; then another minister Shi Shu made a few remarks; Zi Yu, one minister in charge of foreign affairs, made the necessary corrections; and eventually, another minister Zi Chan carefully polished the draft of state documents."

14.9

【原　文】

或问子产。子曰："惠人也。"

问子西。曰："彼哉！彼哉！"

问管仲。曰："人也。夺伯氏骈邑三百，饭疏食，没齿无怨言。"

【汉　译】

有人问孔子，子产其人怎样，孔子说："他是个施惠于民的人。"

又问到子西人怎样，孔子说："他呀！他呀！"

又问管仲人怎样，孔子说："这人呀！他剥夺了伯氏骈邑的三百户封地，伯氏终身只得吃粗粮过活，但到死，他也没有过怨言。"

【英　译】

Someone asked about the character of Zi Chan, a famous statesman at the end of Spring and Autumn Period in China. The Master said, "He was very generous for the common people."

He asked about the character of Zi Xi, one notorious politician in Spring and Autumn Period of China. The Master said, "Why, that guy! That guy!"

That man asked about the character of Guan Zhong, one renowned statesman of State Qi in Spring and Autumn Period of China. The Master said, "He was really formidable. He deprived an old noble family named Bo of three hundred households from their fief in Pian city, and, as a result, all the family were forced to live on the coarse rice. Nevertheless, he did not say a single word of complaint till the end of his life."

14.10

【原　文】

子曰："贫而无怨难，富而无骄易。"

【汉　译】

孔子说："贫穷而没有怨恨，很难做到；富贵而不骄傲，这容易做到。"

【英　译】

The Master said, "It's difficult for one not to make any complaints when poor; yet it's easy for one not to be arrogant when rich."

14.11

【原　文】

子曰："孟公绰为赵、魏老则优，不可以为滕、薛大夫。"

【汉　译】

孔子说："孟公绰若做晋国大夫赵氏、魏氏的家臣，那是才力有余的，但不能让他做滕、薛这样小国的大夫。"

【英　译】

The Master said, "Meng Gongchao would be more than enough as a butler in the great noble family like Zhao or Wei, yet he would not be suitable as a minister in a small state like Teng or Xue."

14.12

【原　文】

子路问成人。子曰："若臧武仲之知，公绰之不欲，卞庄子之勇，冉求之艺，文之以礼乐，亦可以为成人矣。"曰："今之成人者何必然？见利思义，见危授命，久要不忘平生之言，亦可以为成人矣。"

【汉　译】

　　子路问怎样才是完人，孔子说："智慧像臧武仲，清心寡欲像孟公绰，勇敢无畏像卞庄子，多才多艺像冉求，再加以礼乐修养，就可以成为完人了。"孔子又说："现在的完人，何必一定要这样呢？看见财利就想到道义，遇到危险肯献出性命，长久穷困而不忘平生之诺言，这也可以称之为完人。"

【英　译】

　　Zi Lu asked what a perfect man should be like. The Master said, "A man can be considered to be a perfect one if he is as wise as Zang Wuzhong, as desire-free as Meng Gongchao, as brave as Bian Zhuangzi, as accomplished as Ran Qiu, and refined by the rites and music." Then he added, "Nevertheless, there is no need for the present perfect man to have all these things. Such a man may also be called a perfect one if he is able to remember morality and justice when discovering money and goods, risk his life when facing a danger, and not forget his previous promise while permanently living in poverty."

14.13

【原　文】

　　子问公叔文子于公明贾曰："信乎？夫子不言、不笑、不取乎？"公明贾对曰："以告者过也。夫子时然后言，人不厌其言；乐然后笑，人不厌其笑；义然后取，人不厌其取。"子曰："其然？岂其然乎？"

【汉　译】

　　孔子向公明贾问及公叔文子，说："这是真的吗？他老先生不说、不笑、不取钱财。"公明贾答道："那是告诉你的人话说得过分了。他老人家适时才说，所以别人不讨厌他说话；高兴了才笑，所以别人不讨厌他笑；合于义才取，所以别人不厌恶他取。"孔子说："是这样吗？难道真的是这样吗？"

【英 译】

The Master asked Gong Mingjia about his teacher Gong Shu WenZi, "Is it true that your teacher neither spoke nor laughed nor accepted anything from anybody?" Gong Mingjia answered, "The man who told you that actually went too far in his words. As a matter of fact, my teacher spoke at the right moment, and therefore people were not tired of what he said; he laughed when he was really pleased, and therefore people were not tired of hearing his laughter; he accepted what was gained honestly and fairly, and therefore people were not tired of what he accepted." The Master said, "Oh, really? Can it have been so with him?"

14.14

【原 文】

子曰："臧武仲以防求为后于鲁，虽曰不要君，吾不信也。"

【汉 译】

孔子说："臧武仲拿其封地防邑向鲁君请求立他的后代为卿大夫，虽然他说其行为不是要挟君主，我是不相信的。"

【英 译】

The Master said, "Zang Wuzhong utilized his fief of Fang and demanded the Duke of Lu to designate a successor from his descendants. He said that no pressure was put on the Duke, yet I could not trust his words."

14.15

【原 文】

子曰："晋文公谲而不正，齐桓公正而不谲。"

【汉 译】

孔子说："晋文公诡诈而不仗正义，齐桓公仗义而不行诡诈。"

【英　译】

The Master said, "Duke Wen of Jin was wily and failed to uphold justice. Duke Huan of Qi upheld justice and was not crafty."

14.16

【原　文】

子路曰："桓公杀公子纠，召忽死之，管仲不死。"曰："未仁乎？"子曰："桓公九合诸侯，不以兵车，管仲之力也。如其仁，如其仁。"

【汉　译】

子路说："齐桓公杀了其哥哥公子纠，公子纠的家臣召忽自杀以殉，而他的另一家臣管仲却没有死节。"子路接着又说："管仲不能算是仁吧？"孔子说："齐桓公多次召集诸侯共商会盟，不依仗兵车武力，全是管仲的功劳。此乃管仲之仁！此乃管仲之仁！"

【英　译】

Zi Lu said, "Duke Huan of Qi compelled the State of Lu to execute his brother Prince Jiu, Jiu's butler Zhao Hu sacrificed his life for his master, yet Jiu's another butler Guan Zhong failed to do so." He added, "Didn't Guan Zhong lack humanity?" The Master said, "It was due to the strength of Guan Zhong that Duke Huan of Qi was able to assemble the dukes and princes of the Emperor on many occasions rather than resort to force. Such was his humanity. Such was his humanity."

14.17

【原　文】

子贡曰："管仲非仁者与？桓公杀公子纠，不能死，又相之。"子曰："管仲相桓公，霸诸侯，一匡天下，民到于今受其赐。微管仲，吾其被发左衽矣。岂若匹夫匹妇之为谅也，自经于沟渎而莫之知也？"

【汉 译】

子贡说："管仲不是仁人吧？齐桓公杀其主人公子纠，他不为公子纠殉死，还去辅佐桓公。"孔子说："管仲辅佐桓公，称霸诸侯，匡正天下，百姓直到今天还享受其恩惠。倘若没有管仲，我们恐怕要沦为披头散发、衣襟向左边开的落后民族了。哪能要他像普通男女一样，拘泥于小信，自杀于沟渠中，而不为人知呢？"

【英 译】

Zi Gong asked, "Guan Zhong wasn't considered to be a man of humanity, was he? Duke Huan of Qi forced the State of Lu to execute his brother Prince Jiu, Guan Zhong didn't sacrifice his life for his master Prince Jiu, but he became the prime minster of Duke Huan instead."

The Master said, "Guan Zhong assisted Duke Huan in handling state affairs, and therefore Duke Huan was able to dominate all the dukes and princes of the Emperor and unify the country. Up to the present day, the common people still benefit from his great achievements. Actually, without Guan Zhong, we might have been living like the savages with unkempt hair and in barbarian dress, as the front of a Chinese garment folded to the left. Generally, the ordinary men and women always stick to small matters. Would you expect him to die as the common people in a ditch without attracting public attention?"

14.18

【原 文】

公叔文子之臣大夫僎，与文子同升诸公。子闻之，曰："可以为'文'矣。"

【汉 译】

公叔文子的家臣大夫僎，因公叔文子的推荐，与其同升为卫国大臣。孔子听说此事后，说："公叔文子可以称为'文'了。"

【英　译】

Gong-shu Wen-zi had an official called Xun in his household, who was promoted to the rank of minister as high as himself serving in the court of state Wei through his own recommendation. On hearing of this, the Master said, "Gong-shu Wen-zi deserved to be accorded the posthumous title 'Wen' (a cultured man)."

14.19

【原　文】

子言卫灵公之无道也，康子曰："夫如是，奚而不丧？"孔子曰："仲叔圉治宾客，祝鲐治宗庙，王孙贾治军旅。夫如是，奚其丧？"

【汉　译】

孔子说卫灵公乃无道昏君，季康子问道："既如此，为何他还没有败亡呢？"孔子说："有仲叔圉负责接待宾客，有祝鲐主管宗庙祭祀，有王孙贾统领军队。像这样，他又怎会败亡呢？"

【英　译】

On one occasion, the Master was commenting on stupidities and indulgence of Duke Ling of Wei. Hearing of this, Ji Kangzi said, "Since he was so incompetent, why did he not lose his throne?" The Master said, "He had three great and competent ministers: Zhong Shuyu in charge of diplomacy of state, Zhu Tuó in charge of sacrificial affairs of ancestral temple, and Wang Sunjia in charge of military affairs. In this case, how could he lose his throne?"

14.20

【原　文】

子曰："其言之不怍，则为之也难。"

【汉 译】

孔子说："人若说话大言不惭，那他就难把事情做好。"

【英 译】

The Master said, "One does not feel deeply ashamed of his talk, and it is difficult for him to live up to his claim."

14.21

【原 文】

阵成子弑简公。孔子沐浴而朝，告于哀公曰："阵恒弑其君，请讨之。"公曰："告夫三子！"孔子曰："以吾从大夫之后，不敢不告也。君曰'告夫三子'者！"之三子告，不可。孔子曰："以吾从大夫之后，不敢不告也。"

【汉 译】

陈成子杀了齐简公。孔子沐浴斋戒后去朝见鲁哀公，告诉哀公说："陈恒杀了他的国君，请发兵讨伐他。"哀公说："你向三位大夫报告吧！"孔子退朝后说："因为我曾做过大夫，不敢不来报告，君主却说'去报告那三位大夫吧！'"孔子又去向三位大夫报告了，他们都说不能讨伐。孔子说："因为我曾做过大夫，不敢不报告呀！"

【英 译】

Chen Chengzi murdered his master Duke Jian of Qi. On hearing of this, the Master had a bath and went to court and presented himself before Duke Ai of Lu, and said, "Chen Heng has murdered his lord. May I request that the troops be sent to suppress him?" Duke Ai said, "Inform the noble ministers of three families." The Master said, "I was once a minister of the country. According, I think it my duty to inform the lord of this, but he tells me to go and inform the noble ministers of three families." Then the Master went to see the noble ministers of three families and informed them of the matter, but they refused his request. The Master said, "Having been a minister of the country, I consider it my duty to inform you of this."

14.22

【原　文】

子路问事君。子曰："勿欺也，而犯之。"

【汉　译】

子路问怎样侍奉君主。孔子说："不要欺骗他，但可以犯言直谏。"

【英　译】

Zi Lu asked how to serve the lord. The Master said, "Don't say something contrary to your thoughts, but you can bluntly advise your lord despite hurting his dignity."

14.23

【原　文】

子曰："君子上达，小人下达。"

【汉　译】

孔子说："君子日求上进，小人日退沉沦。"

【英　译】

The Master said, "The gentleman goes up while the small man goes down."

14.24

【原　文】

子曰："古之学者为己，今之学者为人。"

【汉　译】

孔子说："古代人学习是为了充实提高自己，现在的人学习是为了给别人看。"

【英　译】

The Master said, "The ancient men learned to improve themselves while the present men learn to impress others."

14.25

【原　文】

蘧伯玉使人于孔子。孔子与之坐而问焉，曰："夫子何为？"对曰："夫子欲寡其过而未能也。"使者出，子曰："使乎！使乎！"

【汉　译】

蘧伯玉派使者来孔子家拜访。孔子让他坐下，问道："老先生近来在做什么呀？"使者回答说："他老人家想减少自己的过失，却没能做到呀。"使者辞别后，孔子说："好一位使者呀！真是一位好使者！"

【英　译】

Qu Boyu sent a messenger to enquire after Confucius. The Master sat with him, and asked, "What is your master doing?" The messenger said, "My master is trying to reduce his faults, but he has been unable to do so." After the messenger left, the Master said, "What a messenger! What a nice messenger!"

14.26

【原　文】

子曰："不在其位，不谋其政。"曾子曰："君子思不出其位。"

【汉　译】

孔子说："不在那个职位上，就不要考虑那职位上的政事。"

曾子说："君子思考问题，不会越出自己的职位。"

【英　译】

The Master said, "A man who he is not in the position should not consider its matter."

Zeng Zi said, "What a gentleman considered is not expected to overstep his authority."

14.27

【原　文】

子曰："君子耻其言而过其行。"

【汉　译】

孔子说："君子以说得多做得少为耻。"

【英　译】

The Master said, "A gentleman is ashamed to say more words than his deeds."

14.28

【原　文】

子曰："君子道者三，我无能焉：仁者不忧，知者不惑，勇者不惧。"子贡曰："夫子自道也。"

【汉　译】

孔子说："君子之道有三条，我一样也没能做到：仁德的人不忧愁，智慧的人不迷惑，勇敢的人不畏惧。"子贡说："这是先生在说自己呢。"

【英　译】

The Master said, "A gentleman adheres to the three principles which I failed to achieve: a man of humanity is free from anxiety; a man of

wisdom is free from doubt; a man of courage is free from fear." Zi Gong
said, "That is just what our master said of himself."

14.29

【原　文】

子贡方人。子曰："赐也贤乎哉？夫我则不暇。"

【汉　译】

子贡说别人的坏话，孔子说："你就那么好吗？我可没有闲暇议
论别人。"

【英　译】

Zi Gong was fond of criticizing others. The Master said, "Ci, are you
really good enough? For myself, I have no more leisure to criticize others."

14.30

【原　文】

子曰："不患人之不己知，患其不能也。"

【汉　译】

孔子说："不要担心别人不知道我，就怕自己没有才能。"

【英　译】

The Master said, "Be not concerned that you are not well known; be
concerned that you lack capabilities."

14.31

【原　文】

子曰："不逆诈，不臆不信，抑亦先觉者，是贤乎！"

【汉　译】

孔子说："不事先猜疑别人欺诈，不随便猜测别人不诚实，但遇到别人欺诈和不诚实时，却能预先察觉，这才是贤人啊！"

【英　译】

The Master said, "One does not suspect deception from others beforehand nor subjectively anticipate dishonesty of others. Nevertheless, he can detect deception and dishonesty from others in advance. Considering that, he deserves a good and wise man."

14.32

【原　文】

微生亩谓孔子曰："丘何为是栖栖者与？无乃为佞乎？"孔子曰："非敢为佞也，疾固也。"

【汉　译】

微生亩对孔子说："孔丘，你为什么这样忙忙碌碌到处游说呢？不是要炫耀你的口才吧？"孔子说："我哪敢炫耀自己的口才呀，只是厌恶那种顽固不通的人。"

【英　译】

Wei Shengmu said to the Master, "Kong Qiu, why are you as busy as a bee here and there? I am afraid that you want to show off your eloquence." Confucius said, "Actually, I don't wish to show off my eloquence. It is just that I detest the obstinate people."

14.33

【原　文】

子曰："骥不称其力，称其德也。"

【汉　译】

孔子说："对于千里马而言，不是称赞它的力气，而是要赞美它的品德。"

【英 译】

The Master said, "A winged steed is eulogized for its good qualities, not for its strength."

14.34

【原 文】

或曰:"以德报怨,何如?"子曰:"何以报德?以直报怨,以德报德。"

【汉 译】

有人说:"用恩德回报怨恨,行吗?"孔子说:"那用什么来回报恩德呢?应该用正直来回报怨恨,用恩德来回报恩德。"

【英 译】

Someone said, "One should return good for evil. How do you think of this statement?" The Master said, "What will we then return for good? We should return justice for evil, and return good for good."

14.35

【原 文】

子曰:"莫我知也夫!"子贡曰:"何为其莫知子也?"子曰:"不怨天,不尤人;下学而上达。知我者其天乎!"

【汉 译】

孔子说:"没有人了解我呀!"子贡说:"为何没有人能了解您呢?"孔子说:"我不埋怨天,也不责怪人;下学通人事,上达知天命。了解我的,大概只有上天吧!"

【英 译】

The Master said, "It's a pity that no one can understand me." Zi

Gong said, "Why does no one understand you?"

The Master said, "I do not grumble against God, nor do I lay the blame upon others. My studies are from learning ways of the world at lower level to understanding God's will at upper level. Ah, perhaps, only God understands me."

14.36

【原　文】

公伯寮愬子路于季孙。子服景伯以告，曰："夫子固有惑志于公伯寮，吾力犹能肆诸市朝。"子曰："道之将行也与，命也；道之将废也与，命也。公伯寮其如命何！"

【汉　译】

公伯寮在季孙氏面前诽谤子路。子服景伯把这事告诉了孔子，说："季孙氏已经被公伯寮的谗言迷惑了，但我的力量还能杀了公伯寮，把他陈尸街头示众。"孔子说："道若能实行，这是天命；道若被废弃，这也是天命。公伯寮能把天命怎么样呢！"

【英　译】

On one occasion, Gong Boliao slandered the Master's disciple Zi Lu before the chief of Ji Sun family. Zi Fu Jing Bo informed the Master of this, and said, "The chief of Ji Sun family is being deluded by Gong Boliao, but I am still strong enough to kill him and expose his corpse on the market." The Master said, "It depends upon God's will whether the Way prevails or not. What can Gong Boliao do against God's will?"

14.37

【原　文】

子曰："贤者辟世，其次辟地，其次辟色，其次辟言。"
子曰："作者七人矣。"

【汉　译】

孔子说："贤人逃避黑暗的现实社会去隐居，次一等的避开一地去另一地方居住，又次一等的看见别人不好的脸色就避开，再次一等的听到别人的恶言才避开。"孔子说："这样做的人已经有七个了。"

【英　译】

The Master said, "A good and wise man would retire from the unjust society; the next one would withdraw from the turbulent country; the next one would try to avoid seeing hostile looks; the next one would try to avoid hearing rude remarks." The Master said, "There are seven men who can do like this."

14.38

【原　文】

子路宿于石门。晨门曰："奚自？"子路曰："自孔氏。"曰："是知其不可而为之者与？"

【汉　译】

子路在石门住了一宿，清晨进城的时候，守门人问道："你来自何方？"子路说："从孔子那里来。"守门人说："是那位明知做不成却还要坚持去做的人吗？"

【英　译】

Zi Lu put up at the Stone Gate one night. On seeing him, the gatekeeper said, "Where do you come from？" Zi Lu said, "I come from the Master." The gatekeeper said, "Oh, isn't it the man who would try to do something impractical？"

14.39

【原　文】

子击磬于卫，有荷蒉而过孔氏之门者，曰："有心哉，击磬乎！"既而曰："鄙哉！硁硁乎！莫己知也，斯己而已矣。深则厉，浅则揭。"子曰:"果哉!末之难矣。"

【汉　译】

孔子在卫国,一天正在家击磬。有个挑着草筐子的人刚好从门前走过,他说道:"这么击磬,是有心事吧!"过了一会儿,他又说:"你这么硁硁作响,也太鄙俗了吧!没有人了解你,自己就独善其身罢了。《诗经》上说,'水深,连衣下水渡河;水浅,撩起衣裳涉水。'——世事深浅,你该知道呀!"孔子说:"真果决呀!我没有话可辩难他。"

【英　译】

On one occasion, the Master was playing an ancient musical instrument called "qing" in the State of Wei when a man carrying a basket passed by the door of his house. On hearing the sound of music, the man said, "Ah, he is not in the mood for beating the musical stone instrument like that." After a little while, he said, "As to the sound of beating the musical stone, how vulgar it sounds! What does it matter if you are unknown? Here are two verses from the Odes, 'Wade the shallow river by lifting clothes; And cross the deep river by wearing clothes.'" On hearing his remarks, the Master said, "What resolute viewpoints! It's difficult for me to argue him down."

14.40

【原　文】

子张曰:"《书》云:'高宗谅阴,三年不言。'何谓也?"子曰:"何必高宗,古之人皆然。君薨,百官总己以听于冢宰三年。"

【汉　译】

子张说:"《尚书》里说:'殷高宗守孝,三年不议政。'这是什么意思呀?"孔子说:"何止高宗一人?古人都是这样:国君死后,继位新君不理朝政,朝廷百官总管自己的职事,听命于宰相三年。"

【英　译】

Zi Zhang said, "*The Book of History* says, 'In order to commemorate his father who had died, Emperor Gao of Yin Dynasty observed three years' silence in the shed of mourning. What does this mean?" The Master said, "Not only Emperor Gao, but also all the ancient people did in the same way. After the sovereign died, all the functionaries continue to take charge of their own offices and received their orders from the prime minister for three years."

14.41

【原　文】

子曰："上好礼，则民易使也。"

【汉　译】

孔子说："在上位的人能恪守礼仪，也就容易役使百姓了。"

【英　译】

The Master said, "So long as the rulers observe the principles of rites, the common people will be easily governed."

14.42

【原　文】

子路问君子。子曰："作己以敬。"

曰："如斯而已乎？"曰："修己以安人。"

曰："如斯而已乎？"曰："修己以安百姓。修己以安百姓，尧舜其犹病诸!"

【汉　译】

子路问怎样做才是个君子。孔子说："自己修身养性，保持谦逊恭敬之心态。"

子路说："这样就够了吗？"孔子说："自己修身养性，可使亲友享安乐。"

子路又问："这样就够了吗？"孔子说："自己修身养性，可使百姓享安乐。自己修身养性使百姓得到安乐，尧、舜还难以做到呢!"

【英 译】

Zi Lu asked about a good and wise man. The Master said, "He often cultivates himself and retains a respectful attitude towards others."

Zi Lu said, "Is that all?" The Master said, "He often cultivates himself and thereby brings the happiness for others."

Zi Lu said, "Is that all?" The Master said, "He often cultivates himself and thereby brings the happiness for the common people. As regards this point, even the ancient great emperors Yao and Shun find it difficult to come up to this standard."

14.43

【原 文】

原壤夷俟。子曰："幼而不孙弟，长而无述焉，老而不死，是为贼。"以杖叩其胫。

【汉 译】

原壤两腿叉开平身，坐着等孔子。孔子说："你年幼时不知孝悌，长大了没有成就，老了还不死，简直是个害人虫！"说着就用拐杖敲他的小腿。

【英 译】

On one occasion, Yuan Rang was waiting for the Master, squatting on his heels. The Master then said, "You showed neither modesty nor deference in your youth; you had nothing accomplished in manhood; you live on without purpose in old age. What a real pest you are!" Then the Master hit him on the shanks with his staff.

14.44

【原 文】

阙党童子将命，或问之曰："益者与?"子曰："吾见其居于位也，见其与先生并行也。非求益者也，欲速成者也。"

【汉　译】

　　阙党之地有一童子，来给孔子传话。有人问道："这是个求上进的孩子吗？"孔子说："我见他坐在成年人的位子上，又见他和长辈并肩而行。可见，这孩子不是想求上进，而是一个急于求成的人。"

【英　译】

　　There was a lad in Que Dang, who took a message for the Master. Someone then asked him, "Does the boy strive to improve his learning?" The Master said, "I've observed him sitting in the place of an adult and walking side by side with his seniors. Obviously, he is not the one who strives to improve his learning, but the one who is eager to become a grown-up."

卫灵公篇第十五

15.1

【原　文】

卫灵公问陈于孔子。孔子对曰："俎豆之事，则尝闻之矣；军旅之事，未之学也。"明日遂行。

【汉　译】

卫灵公向孔子问军队布阵之事，孔子回答说："礼仪方面的事，我曾听说过一些；军事方面的问题，我却没有学习过。" 第二天，孔子便离开了卫国。

【英　译】

Duke Ling of Wei asked the Master about the battle array of troops. The Master answered, "I've heard of something about the sacrificial rites, yet I've never learned the matter of military affairs." The next day he left the state of Wei.

15.2

【原　文】

在陈绝粮，从者病，莫能兴。子路愠见曰："君子亦有穷乎？"子曰："君子固穷，小人穷斯滥矣。"

【汉　译】

孔子在陈国粮食断绝了，随行的弟子都饿病了，站不起来。子路满脸不高兴，来见孔子，说道："君子也有穷困潦倒的时候吗？"孔子说："君子穷困时，仍能恪尽操守；小人一旦贫穷，便胡作非为了。"

【英　译】

The Master on one occasion arrived in the state Chen, and having run out of food, his disciples got so hungry that they couldn't rise to their feet. Discontented, Zi Lu said to the Master, "A good and wise man, can he also be penniless and frustrated?" The Master said, "A good and wise man can still behave with integrity even in poverty, while a small man will commit all kinds of outrages once in poverty."

15.3

【原　文】

子曰："赐也，女以予为多学而识之者与？"对曰："然，非与？"曰："非也，予一以贯之。"

【汉　译】

孔子说："赐呀，你以为我是学得多又能都记得住吗？"子贡答道："是呀！难道不是吗？"孔子说："不是的。在此多学中，我有一种办法能把零散的记忆贯穿起来。"

【英　译】

The Master once said to his disciple, "Ci, do you think that I possess wide learning and a powerful memory?" Zi Gong replied, "Yes, but is it not so?" The Master then said, "No. I grasp all my knowledge by one principle."

15.4

【原　文】

子曰："由！知德者鲜矣。"

【汉　译】

孔子说："由呀，知道德的人，确实太少了。"

【英　译】

　　The Master said to his disciple, "You, very few people understand virtue now."

15.5

【原　文】

　　子曰："无为而治者，其舜也与？夫何为哉？恭己正南面而已矣。"

【汉　译】

　　孔子说："能够无为而治的先皇，大概只有舜了吧？他做了些什么呢？他只是恭谨端正地坐在南面天子之位罢了。"

【英　译】

　　The Master said, "Presumably it's only the ancient Emperor Shun who could govern his country by non-action. What did he do? He just occupied the throne uprightly and reverentially."

15.6

【原　文】

　　子张问行。子曰："言忠信，行笃敬，虽蛮貊之邦，行矣。言不忠信，行不笃敬，虽州里，行乎哉？立则见其参于前也，在舆则见其倚于衡也，夫然后行。"子张书诸绅。

【汉　译】

　　子张问怎样才能使自己行为通达。孔子说："说话忠诚守信，行事笃实严谨，即使到了未开化的落后地区，也能行得通。若说话不忠信，行事不笃敬，就是在本乡本土，又怎能行得通呢？站立时仿佛看见'忠信笃敬'这几个字就在我们眼前，在车上又好似看见这几个字在车前横木上，这样才能使自己行为通达。"子张把孔子这些话写在束腰间的大带上。

【英 译】

Zi Zhang asked how to get along well with people. The Master said, "If you keep your word sincerely and do your deed earnestly, you will get along well with others even among the uncivilized tribes. Otherwise, if you say your words insincerely and do your deeds inattentively, how will you be able to get along well with others even in your hometown? While standing, you will be able to see these words before you; while sitting in a carriage, you will be able to see them inscribed on the wooden handlebar. If so, you will get along well with others." Zi Zhang then wrote these words on his girdle.

15.7

【原 文】

子曰："直哉，史鱼！邦有道，如矢；邦无道，如矢。君子哉，蘧伯玉！邦有道，则仕；邦无道，则可卷而怀之。"

【汉 译】

孔子说："史鱼，多么正直啊！国家政治清明时，他像箭一样刚直；国家政治黑暗时，他也像箭一样刚直。蘧伯玉，乃真君子啊！国家政治清明时，他就出来做官；国家政治黑暗时，他就退隐山林。"

【英 译】

The Master said, "How straightforward Shi Yu was! When there were justice and order prevailing in the state, he served as a straight arrow in the government of his country; yet when there were no justice and order in the state, he still served as a straight arrow in the government of his country. What a good and wise man Ju Boyu was! When there were justice and order prevailing in the state, he served as an official in the government of his country; yet when there were no justice and order in the state, he quit working to retire from public life."

15.8

【原　文】

子曰："可与言而不与之言，失人；不可与言而与之言，失言。知者不失人，亦不失言。"

【汉　译】

孔子说："可以和他说话，而不和他讲，这是错失人；不可以和他说话，却同他讲了，这叫说话失口。智慧之人不错失人，也不说话失口。"

【英　译】

The Master said, "You are supposed to talk to a man, but you do not talk to him, and then you will lose the worthy man. Otherwise, you are not supposed to talk to a man, yet you talk to him, and then you will waste your words. A man of wisdom will neither lose a worthy man nor waste his words."

15.9

【原　文】

子曰："志士仁人，无求生以害仁，有杀身以成仁。"

【汉　译】

孔子说："志士仁人，决不苟且偷生而妨害仁道，宁愿杀身而成就仁道。"

【英　译】

The Master said, "A man of aspirations and virtue will make no attempt to save his life but sacrifice his life to achieve his virtue and morality."

15.10

【原　文】

子贡问为仁。子曰："工欲善其事，必先利其器。居是邦也，事其大夫之贤者，友其士之仁者。"

【汉　译】

　　子贡问如何行仁道。孔子说："工匠要想把自己的活儿做好，一定要把他用的工具磨锋利。居住在这个国家，就要侍奉国内大夫中的贤人，并与士人中的仁人交朋友。"

【英　译】

　　ZI Gong asked about the practice of humanity. The Master said, "A craftsman who wants to do his work well must first sharpen his own tools. Living in this state, you should serve the grand ministers and cultivate the friendship of the good scholars."

15.11

【原　文】

　　颜渊问为邦。子曰："行夏之时，乘殷之辂，服周之冕，乐则韶舞。放郑声，远佞人。郑声淫，佞人殆。"

【汉　译】

　　颜渊问治国之道。孔子说："推行夏朝的历法，乘商朝的车子，戴周朝的礼帽，演奏韶乐和武乐，舍弃郑国音乐，疏远小人。因郑国音乐淫靡，谄媚小人危险。"

【英　译】

　　Yan Yuan asked how to govern a state. The Master said, "Use the calendar of the Xia dynasty, take the carriage of the Yin dynasty, wear the hats of the Zhou dynasty, play the ancient music of Emperor Shun and the Martial King, prohibit the popular songs of the Zheng state which are licentious, and become estranged from the flatterers who are dangerous."

15.12

【原　文】

　　子曰："人无远虑，必有近忧。"

【汉　译】

孔子说："人若没有长远的打算，必定会有眼前的忧虑。"

【英　译】

The Master said, "If he takes no thought for the remote future, a man will undoubtedly be beset by worries at hand."

15.13

【原　文】

子曰："已矣乎！吾未见好德如好色者也。"

【汉　译】

孔子说："算了吧！我还没见过有谁能像好色一样好德。"

【英　译】

The Master said, "Alas! I've never met a man who loves morality more than beauty."

15.14

【原　文】

子曰："臧文仲其窃位者与！知柳下惠之贤而不与立也。"

【汉　译】

孔子说："臧文仲是个窃居官位的人吧！他明知柳下惠贤良，却不举荐他做官。"

【英　译】

The Master said, "Zang Wenzhong was a man who had stolen his position. He knew well that Liu Xiahui had the talents and virtues, but he would not recommend him to serve as official in the court."

15.15

【原　文】

子曰："躬自厚而薄责于人，则远怨矣。"

【汉　译】

孔子说："多责问自己，少责备别人，就可以避免怨恨了。"

【英　译】

The Master said, "If he is strict with himself and lenient with others, a man will be far from their complaints."

15.16

【原　文】

子曰："不曰'如之何，如之何'者，吾末如之何也已矣。"

【汉　译】

孔子说："从不说'怎么办，怎么办'的人，我也不知道该拿他怎么办。"

【英　译】

The Master said, "A man never says to himself 'What to do? What to do?' I really do not know what I can do with such a man."

15.17

【原　文】

子曰："群居终日，言不及义，好行小慧，难矣哉！"

【汉　译】

孔子说："整天扎堆聊天，言谈不涉及道义，喜好耍小聪明，这种人很难有出息啊！"

【英 译】

The Master said, "Some people gather together all day long without talking about morality and justice but try to show off their cleverness in trivial matters. There is no future for them."

15.18

【原 文】

子曰："君子义以为质，礼以行之，孙以出之，信以成之。君子哉！"

【汉 译】

孔子说："君子以义为行事之本质，以礼仪来实行义，以谦逊之言语表达义，以诚信来完成义。这样才是个君子啊！"

【英 译】

The Master said, "A good and wise man treats righteousness as the substance of his being; he puts it into practice by the rules of rites; he gives it expression with modesty; and he accomplishes it with sincerity. Such is a really good and rise man!"

15.19

【原 文】

子曰："君子病无能焉，不病人之不己知也。"

【汉 译】

孔子说："君子只担忧自己没才能，不担心别人不知道自己。"

【英 译】

The Master said, "A good and wise man regrets that he lacks ability, but he does not regret that others do not take notice of him."

15.20

【原　文】

　　子曰："君子疾没世而名不称焉。"

【汉　译】

　　孔子说："君子担心死后其名声不为人所称颂。"

【英　译】

　　The Master said, "A good and wise man is afraid of not leaving a name behind after his death."

15.21

【原　文】

　　子曰："君子求诸己，小人求诸人。"

【汉　译】

　　孔子说："君子求之于己，小人求之于人。"

【英　译】

　　The Master said, "A good and wise man relies on himself while a small man relies on others."

15.22

【原　文】

　　子曰："君子矜而不争，群而不党。"

【汉　译】

　　孔子说："君子庄重而不与人争执，合群而不与人相互勾结。"

【英　译】

　　The Master said, "A good and wise man is dignified but does not like to argue with others; he is social but does not gang up for selfish purposes."

15.23

【原　文】

子曰："君子不以言举人，不以人废言。"

【汉　译】

孔子说："君子不因一人说话好听就举荐他，也不因其为人不好就否定他讲的好话。"

【英　译】

The Master said, "A good and wise man will not recommend a man on account of his good words, nor reject his good words because of his bad behavior."

15.24

【原　文】

子贡问曰："有一言而可以终身行之者乎？"子曰："其恕乎！己所不欲，勿施于人。"

【汉　译】

子贡问道："有没有一个字可以终身奉行的呢？"孔子说："那就是恕吧！自己所不愿意要的，就不要强加给别人。"

【英　译】

Zi Gong asked, "Is there a single word that we can follow throughout the whole life?" The Master said, "That's the word 'forgiveness'! Do not do to others what you do not wish them to do to you."

15.25

【原　文】

子曰："吾之于人也，谁毁谁誉？如有所誉者，其有所试矣。斯民也，三代之所以直道而行也。"

【汉　译】

孔子说："我评论人时，诋毁过谁？称赞过谁？假如有我称赞过的，那也是经过考验的。夏、商、周三代人正是这样，所以这三个朝代都能在正道上行事。"

【英　译】

The Master said, "In my judgment of others, is there anyone I once defamed or praised? If there is a man I once praised, I must have tested him and carefully weighed my judgment. The people, in the three ancient dynasties of Xia and Shang and Zhou, behaved just like this. Such is a straightforward way by which they could successfully handle their affairs."

15.26

【原　文】

子曰："吾犹及史之阙文也，有马者借人乘之，今亡矣夫！"

【汉　译】

孔子说："我还能看到史书上有存疑之处，有马的人将马借给别人骑，现如今这些都没有了！"

【英　译】

The Master said, "In my early days, I found that the historiographer, if in doubt, left a blank in his text, and a horseman lent his horse to another man. Nowadays, there are no such cases."

15.27

【原　文】

子曰："巧言乱德。小不忍则乱大谋。"

【汉　译】

孔子说："花言巧语会败坏人的品德。小处不能忍，就会坏大事。"

【英　译】

The Master said, "Flattery will ruin one's virtue; petty impatience will spoil the main event."

15.28

【原　文】

子曰："众恶之，必察焉；众好之，必察焉。"

【汉　译】

孔子说："人人都厌恶之人，一定要去考察一番；人人都喜欢的人，也一定要去考察一下。"

【英　译】

The Master said, "If a man is hated by all the people, it is imperative to find out why people dislike him. If a man is liked by all, it is still essential to find out why people like him."

15.29

【原　文】

子曰："人能弘道，非道弘人。"

【汉　译】

孔子说："人能把道发扬光大，道却不能弘大人。"

【英　译】

The Master said, "It is man who can improve the law, but not the law that can enhance man."

15.30

【原　文】

子曰："过而不改，是谓过矣。"

【汉 译】

孔子说："犯了过错而不改正，这才真叫过错了。"

【英 译】

The Master said, "A man refused to mend his fault, though he made a fault. That's really a fault for him."

15.31

【原 文】

子曰："吾尝终日不食，终夜不寝，以思，无益，不如学也。"

【汉 译】

孔子说："我曾经整天不吃饭，整夜不睡觉，尽心思考，依然没有收益，不如去学习的好。"

【英 译】

The Master said, "I once spent a whole day and a whole night in reflecting, without taking any food and going to bed. It was of no use. I found it better to learn knowledge from the books."

15.32

【原 文】

子曰："君子谋道不谋食。耕也，馁在其中矣；学也，禄在其中矣。君子忧道不忧贫。"

【汉 译】

孔子说："君子用心求道，而不谋求衣食。耕田，也难免饿肚皮；学习，能够得到俸禄。君子为求道而忧虑，不会为贫穷而发愁。"

【英 译】

The Master said, "A good and wise man is engaged in seeking for truth, not making a mere living. Farming, he even suffers from starvation from time to time; learning, he is able to obtain the salary of an official. Therefore, a good and wise man just worries about truth, not about poverty."

15.33

【原　文】

子曰:"知及之,仁不能守之,虽得之,必失之。知及之,仁能守之,不庄以莅之,则民不敬。知及之,仁能守之,庄以莅之,动之不以礼,未善也。"

【汉　译】

孔子说:"靠智慧得到的,不以仁德保持它,即使得到了,也一定会失去的。靠智慧得到的,以仁德保持它,而不以庄重的态度对待,老百姓也不会敬服。靠智慧得到的,以仁德保持它,又能以庄重的态度对待,但不用礼法动员百姓,也还是不够完善的。"

【英　译】

The Master said, "A man is wise sufficient to gain it, but not benevolent enough to preserve it, he will lose what is obtained. A man is wise sufficient to gain it and benevolent enough to preserve it, yet he will not inspire respect in the people if he rules them without dignity. A man is wise sufficient to gain it and benevolent enough to preserve it, and governing without dignity, he is not yet perfect if he does not rule the people in accordance with the rules of rites."

15.34

【原　文】

子曰:"君子不可小知而可大受也,小人不可大受而可小知也。"

【汉　译】

孔子说:"君子不可以小事考验,但可委以重任;小人不可委以重任,而可以小事去考察他。"

【英　译】

The Master said, "A good and wise man cannot be judged on the basis of the small matters, but he can be entrusted with the great task. A small man can not he entrusted with the great task, but he can be judged by the small matters."

15.35

【原　文】

子曰："民之于仁也，甚于水火。水火，吾见蹈而死者矣，未见蹈仁而死者也。"

【汉　译】

孔子说："百姓对于仁德，比对于水火更需求。我只见过人蹈火溺水而死的，却没见过实行仁德而死去的。"

【英　译】

The Master said, "The common people need humanity more than water and fire. I have seen people drown in water or falling into fire, but I've never seen them die from carrying out humanity."

15.36

【原　文】

子曰："当仁，不让于师。"

【汉　译】

孔子说："行仁之事，在老师面前也不必谦让。"

【英　译】

The Master said, "As for the question of carrying out humanity, a man should not defer to his teacher."

15.37

【原　文】

　　子曰："君子贞而不谅。"

【汉　译】

　　孔子说："君子固守正道，而不拘泥于小信用。"

【英　译】

　　The Master said, "A good and wise man is faithful to the principles, but not obstinate in the minor credits."

15.38

【原　文】

　　子曰："事君，敬其事而后其食。"

【汉　译】

　　孔子说："侍奉君主，应忠于职守善其事，然后再谈个人俸禄。"

【英　译】

　　The Master said, "In serving the lord, a man should be devoted to his duty before considering his salary."

15.39

【原　文】

　　子曰："有教无类。"

【汉　译】

　　孔子说："人人我都可以教化，没有贫富贵贱之分。"

【英　译】

　　The Master said, "As far as I am concerned, there is no distinction of classes among the educated people."

15.40

【原　文】

子曰："道不同，不相为谋。"

【汉　译】

孔子说："人若思想主张不同，便无法在一起谋事。"

【英　译】

The Master said, "Having entirely different principles, men will not consider acting together."

15.41

【原　文】

子曰："辞达而已矣。"

【汉　译】

孔子说："言辞能把意思表达清楚就行了。"

【英　译】

The Master said, "It is wise that one's language should be intelligible to the people."

15.42

【原　文】

　　师冕见，及阶，子曰："阶也。"及席，子曰："席也。"皆坐，子告之曰："某在斯，某在斯。"师冕出，子张问曰："与师言之道与?"子曰："然，固相师之道也。"

【汉　译】

　　师冕来见孔子，走到台阶前，孔子说："这儿是台阶。"走到坐席旁，孔子说："这儿是坐席。"大家坐下后，孔子对师冕说："某人坐在这边，某人坐在那边。"师冕走后，子张问道："这就是同乐师说话的方式吗?"孔子说："是的，这就是一种帮助盲人的方式呀!"

【英 译】

On one occasion, a blind musician Mian called on the Master. When he came to the steps of the house, the Master said to him, "Here are the steps." When he came to the mat for him to sit, the Master said again, "Here is the mat." After everyone was seated, the Master said to him, "So-and-so is here, and so-and-so is over there." After the blind musician left, a disciple Zi Zhang asked the Master, "Is that the way to talk to a great musician?" The Master said, "Yes, that's a way to help a blind musician."

季氏篇第十六

16.1

【原　文】

　　季氏将伐颛臾。冉有、季路见于孔子曰："季氏将有事于颛臾。"孔子曰："求！无乃尔是过与？夫颛臾，昔者先王以为东蒙主，且在邦域之中矣，是社稷之臣也，何以伐为？"

　　冉有曰："夫子欲之，吾二臣者皆不欲也。"孔子曰："求！周任有言曰：'陈力就列，不能者止。'危而不持，颠而不扶，则将焉用彼相矣？且尔言过矣！虎兕出于柙，龟玉毁于椟中，是谁之过与？"

　　冉有曰："今夫颛臾，固而近于费。今不取，后世必为子孙忧。"

　　孔子曰："求！君子疾夫舍曰欲之，而必为之辞。丘也闻有国有家者，不患寡而患不均，不患贫而患不安。盖均无贫，和无寡，安无倾。夫如是，故远人不服，则修文德以来之。既来之，则安之。今由与求也，相夫子，远人不服而不能来也，邦分崩离析而不能守也，而谋动干戈于邦内。吾恐季孙之忧，不在颛臾，而在萧墙之内也。"

【汉　译】

　　季氏要兴兵讨伐颛臾，冉有和季路去见孔子，说："季氏要对颛臾用兵了。"孔子说："求呀！这怕是你的过失吧？那颛臾，从前先王封它为东蒙山的主祭，况且它在鲁国境内，是鲁国的臣属呀，为何要攻打它呢？"

　　冉有说："这是季老夫子要这样做的，我们两人都不想这样做。"孔子说："求呀！从前周任曾说过：'能施展自己的才能，则就其职位；若不能胜任，就应该辞职。'你的主子遇有危险，你不去拉他一把；他要跌倒了，也不去扶他一下，那要你们辅佐的人干什么呢？而且你的话也说错了。老虎、野牛从笼子里逸出为患，龟甲、玉器在匣子里毁坏了，这是谁的过错呢？"

冉有说："如今颛臾城郭坚固，而且离费邑又很近。若现在不夺取它，将来必定成为后代子孙的忧患。"孔子说："求呀！君子讨厌那种故意不说自己想干什么，而非要找个说法做借口的人。我听说，对于国君和大夫而言，不愁国家财富少，就怕分配不均；不愁百姓贫穷，就怕他们不安分。财富分配均等了，就无所谓贫穷；百姓能和睦相处，就无所谓寡；百姓能安分守己，国家就无倾覆之患。正因为这样，所以远方之人若还不归服，就整治礼乐和仁政来招引他们。既然他们来了，就把他们安顿好。仲由和冉求，你们两人现在辅佐季氏，远方之人不归服，你们却不能把他们招来；国家分崩离析，你们不能好好防守，却图谋在国内大动干戈。我怕季孙的忧虑不在颛臾，而在国君宫室内部吧？"

【英　译】

The head of Ji family was preparing to attack a small principality called Zhuan Yu. Two disciples, Ran You and Zi Lu came to see the Master and said, "Our chief is going to launch an attack on Zhuan Yu." The Master said, "Ran Qiu, is it not due to your fault? Zhuan Yu was once appointed by the ancient kings to preside over the ceremony of offering sacrifices to the Dong Meng Mountain. Besides, it lies within the country Lu and a vassal state to safeguard our land. I'd like to know the reason why he is going to attack it."

Ran You said, "It is our master Ji Shi who wishes to attack Zhuan Yu. Neither of us agrees with him, but we are only his servants." The Master then said, "Qiu, as the saying of Zhou Ren goes, 'You should take the office if you can display your abilities. Or else, you should resign if you can't.' When your master is in danger, you won't give him a hand; when your master falls down, you won't prop him up. What's the use of the assistant to his master? Besides, what you said is totally wrong. If a tiger or a wild ox escapes from its cage, or if a tortoise shell or a precious gem is broken in its casket, who will be responsible for such a fault?"

Ran You said, "Now Zhuan Yu is a strongly fortified principality and is located very close to our most important fief of Fei. If it is not captured now, I'm afraid that it will undoubtedly become a source of anxiety and trouble for the descendents of our master in the future."

The Master said, "Ran Qiu, a good and wise man detests those who try to find a plausible pretext rather than saying what they want to do. I've heard that the head of a state or a noble family should not worry about having scarce wealth but about unequal distribution of wealth, not about poverty but about unrest. If there is equal distribution of wealth, there will be no poverty; if people live together in perfect harmony, there will be no sparseness of population; if people abide by law and behave themselves, there will be no downfall and dissolution of a state. For this reason, if the distant people do not give in, the moral education should be improved to attract them. And they should be comfortably installed after their arrival. At present, Zi Lu and Ran You, while assisting your chief, you can not attract the distant people who do not submit to him; when your country is on the verge of disintegration, you can do nothing to safeguard it but instead plan to resort to force within the state. I'm afraid that the danger of Ji family may not arise from the small principality Zhuan Yu but from within the walls of your chief's own palace."

16.2

【原　文】

孔子曰："天下有道，则礼乐征伐自天子出；天下无道，则礼乐征伐自诸侯出。自诸侯出，盖十世希不失矣；自大夫出，五世希不失矣；陪臣执国命，三世希不失矣。天下有道，则政不在大夫。天下有道，则庶人不议。"

【汉　译】

孔子说："国家政治清明时，礼乐制度和征伐号令均由天子决定；国家政治黑暗时，礼乐制度和征伐号令就由诸侯决定。由诸侯决定，大概传到十代很少有不失掉天下的；由大夫决定，传到五代很少有不失掉天下的；由家臣把持国家朝政，传到三代很少有不失掉天下的。国家政治清明，政权就不会由大夫把持。国家政治清明，老百姓就不会议论朝政了。"

【英　译】

The Master said,"When there are order and justice in the government of a country, the decrees of ritual and music and declaration of war are issued by the sovereign. When there are disorder and injustice in the government of a country, the decrees of ritual and music and declaration of war are issued by the princes. If the official orders issued by the princes, their rule could be maintained for ten generations at most; if the official orders issued by the ministers, their rule could be maintained for five generations at most; if the official orders issued by the subordinate officers, their rule could be maintained for three generations at most. When there are order and justice in the government of a country, the country will not be governed by the subordinate officers; when there are order and justice in the government of a country, the common people will not have disputes over the state affairs."

16.3

【原　文】

孔子曰："禄之去公室五世矣，政逮于大夫四世矣，故夫三桓之子孙微矣。"

【汉　译】

孔子说："鲁君丧失爵禄之权，已经有五代了；政权落到大夫手中，已经有四代了。所以，三桓的子孙现在也衰微了。"

【英　译】

The Master said,"It is five generations since the Ducal House has lost his political power. It is four generations since the political power has been in the hands of ministers. For this reason, the descendants of the three Huan families have lost their power."

16.4

【原 文】

孔子曰："益者三友，损者三友。友直，友谅，友多闻，益矣。友便辟，友善柔，友便佞，损矣。"

【汉 译】

孔子说："有益的朋友有三类，有害的朋友也有三类。和正直的人交朋友，和守信的人交朋友，和见识广的人交朋友，是有好处的。和善于装饰外表的人交朋友，和工于媚悦的面善之人交朋友，和惯于花言巧语的人交朋友，是有害处的。"

【英 译】

The Master said, "One stands to benefit from three kinds of friends. Similarly, he stands to lose from three kinds of other friends. It will do him good to make friends with the upright, the trustworthy and the well-informed people. It will do him harm to make friends with the insincere, the fawning and the plausible people."

16.5

【原 文】

孔子曰："益者三乐，损者三乐。乐节礼乐，乐道人之善，乐多贤友，益矣。乐骄乐，乐佚游，乐宴乐，损矣。"

【汉 译】

孔子说："有益于人的快乐有三种，有害于人的快乐亦有三种。以礼乐节制自己的言行为乐，以赞扬别人的好处为乐，以多结交好朋友为乐，这是有益处的。以骄纵放肆为乐，以纵情游荡为乐，以宴饮纵欲为乐，这是有害处的。"

【英 译】

The Master said, "One stands to benefit from three kinds of pleasures. Similarly, he stands to lose from three other kinds of pleasures. Three pleasures will do him good: delight in his acts constrained from ritual and music, in praising the excellent qualities of others and in making many good friends. Three other pleasures will do him harm: delight in showing arrogance, in idle extravagance and in the most sumptuous dinner."

16.6

【原　文】

孔子曰："侍于君子有三愆：言未及之而言，谓之躁；言及之而不言，谓之隐；未见颜色而言，谓之瞽。"

【汉　译】

孔子说："陪君子说话，易犯三种过失：没轮到你说话时，就抢先发言了，这叫急躁；该你说话时而不说，这叫隐匿；不看君子的脸色就随便说话，这叫睁眼瞎子。"

【英　译】

The Master said, "When in the presence of his superior, one is liable to make three mistakes. It is called reckless for him to speak out when not called on to speak; it is called cagey for him to keep silence when called on to speak; it is called blind for him to speak out without observing the expression on the face of his superior."

16.7

【原　文】

孔子曰："君子有三戒：少之时，血气未定，戒之在色；及其壮也，血气方刚，戒之在斗；及其老也，血气既衰，戒之在得。"

【汉　译】

孔子说："君子有三戒：年轻时，血气未定，当戒迷恋女色；壮年时，血气方刚，当戒争强好斗；年老了，血气已衰，当戒贪得无厌。"

【英 译】

The Master said, "A wise man should beware of three things in his whole life. He should beware of lust as being impulsive in youth; he should beware of strife in adult life when being full of vigor; he should beware of acquisitiveness late in life when his vitality being in decay."

16.8

【原 文】

孔子曰："君子有三畏：畏天命，畏大人，畏圣人之言。小人不知天命而不畏也，狎大人，侮圣人之言。"

【汉 译】

孔子说："君子有三件事心存敬畏：一是敬畏天命，二是敬畏身居高位之人，三是敬畏圣人的话。小人不知有天命，因而也不敬畏，轻慢高位之人，轻侮圣人之言。"

【英 译】

The Master said, "A good and wise man is in awe of three things. He stands in awe of Heaven's will; he stands in awe of the great men; he stands in awe of the sage's words. The small man does not stand in awe of Heaven's will as he knows nothing about it. He treats the great men with disrespect, and he despises the sage's words."

16.9

【原 文】

孔子曰："生而知之者，上也；学而知之者，次也；困而学之，又其次也；困而不学，民斯为下矣。"

【汉 译】

孔子说："生来就知道的，是上等人；学了才知道的，是次一等；遇到了困难才知道要学的，是又次一等；遇到了困难还不学的，那就是最下等人。"

【英 译】

The Master said, "Those who are born with knowledge are the highest class of people. Those who acquire knowledge by learning are the next class of people. Those who strive to learn in awkward difficulties are the next class of people again. The common people, who will not strive to learn in awkward difficulties, are the lowest class of people."

16.10

【原 文】

孔子曰："君子有九思：视思明，听思聪，色思温，貌思恭，言思忠，事思敬，疑思问，忿思难，见得思义。"

【汉 译】

孔子说："君子有九件事要考虑：看的时候，要考虑是否看明白了；听的时候，要考虑是否听清楚了；自己的脸色，要考虑是否温和；容貌态度，要考虑是否谦恭；说话，要考虑是否诚实；做事，要考虑是否敬业；遇到疑问，要考虑向别人请教；愤怒时，要考虑是否有后患；见有可得之物，要考虑是否应该得到。"

【英 译】

The Master said, "A wise man is expected to consider nine things. He should consider whether to see clearly in the use of his eyes, to hear distinctly in the use of his ears, to be mild in the expression of his look, to be respectful in the facial expression and his manner, to be sincere in what he says, to be earnest in what he does, to seek for information when in doubt, to have serious consequences when in anger, and to have what is right in sight of gain."

16.11

【原 文】

孔子曰："见善如不及，见不善如探汤。吾见其人矣，吾闻其语矣。隐居以求其志，行义以达其道。吾闻其语矣，未见其人也。"

【汉　译】

孔子说："看见好的行为，唯恐赶不上；看见不好的，就好像把手伸到沸水里一样，赶紧避开。这样的人我见过，这样的话我也听过。在隐居中能保全平生志向，坚守道义以实现自己的主张。这样的话我听到过，这样的人我却没有见过。"

【英　译】

The Master said, "When seeing what is good, a man would try to do it; when seeing what is bad, a man would try to avoid it as if he put his hands into scalding water and draw back immediately. I have met such a man, and I have heard of such a claim. When leading a secluded life, a man would achieve his aims; when practising righteousness, a man would carry out his principles. I have heard of such a claim, but I have never met such a man."

16.12

【原　文】

齐景公有马千驷，死之日，民无德而称焉。伯夷、叔齐饿于首阳之下，民到于今称之。其斯之谓与？

【汉　译】

齐景公有四千匹马，可他富而无德，到他死时，百姓觉得他没什么可称道的。伯夷、叔齐饿死在首阳山下，百姓到今天还在称颂他们。大概就是这个意思吧？

【英　译】

Duke Jing of the state Qi had a thousand chariots with four horses each during his lifetime, but the common people had not a good word to praise him on the day of his death. Bo Yi and Shu Qi, two ancient loyal brothers, were starved to death at the foot of Mount Shou Yang, but the common people still bear their virtue in mind to this day. Is this probably not what is meant?

16.13

【原 文】

陈亢问于伯鱼曰："子亦有异闻乎？"对曰："未也。尝独立，鲤趋而过庭。曰：'学诗乎？'对曰：'未也。''不学诗，无以言。'鲤退而学诗。他日，又独立，鲤趋而过庭。曰：'学礼乎？'对曰：'未也。''不学礼，无以立。'鲤退而学礼。闻斯二者。"陈亢退而喜曰："问一得三：闻诗，闻礼，又闻君子之远其子也。"

【汉 译】

陈亢向伯鱼问道："你从你父亲那里听到些特别的教诲吗？"伯鱼回答说："没有呀！有一次，我父亲一人站在堂上，我快步从中庭走过，他问我：'你学过诗没有？'我回答说：'还没有。'我父亲说：'不学诗，就不懂得如何讲话。'我回去后便学诗。又一次，我父亲又独自一人站在堂上，我又快步从中庭走过，他问我：'你学过礼没有吗？'我回答说：'还没有。'我父亲说：'不学礼，就不懂得如何立身。'我回去后便学礼。我就听到过他这两次教诲。"陈亢回去后，高兴地说："我只问了一个问题，竟有三个收获：知道了该学诗，知道了该学礼，知道了君子对自己的儿子也不偏爱。"

【英 译】

On one occasion, Chen Gang asked the Master's son Bo Yu, "Have you been given any special lesson by your father?" Bo Yu said, "No, I have not. Once my father was standing alone in the hall, and I happened to pass by quickly, he said to me, 'Have you ever studied the poetry?' I answered, 'No, I have not.' Then he said, 'If you don't study the poetry, you can not speak very well.' I retired and gave myself to studying the poetry. On another occasion, my father was again standing alone in the hall, and I happened to pass by quickly, he said to me, 'Have you studied the rituals?' I answered, 'No, I have not.' Then he said, 'If you don't study the rituals, you can not get established in society.' I retired and gave

myself to studying the rituals. I've had only two lessons from my father."
Delighted, Chen Gang retired and said, "I've just asked one thing, but I have learned three things. I have learnt the importance of studying the poetry and rituals, and also that a good and wise man does not have any particular preference for his own son."

16.14

【原　文】

邦君之妻，君称之曰"夫人"，夫人自称曰"小童"；邦人称之曰"君夫人"，称诸异邦曰"寡小君"；异邦人称之亦曰"君夫人"。

【汉　译】

国君的妻子，国君称她为"夫人"，她对国君自称"小童"；国内人称她为"君夫人"，对别国人则称她为"寡小君"；别国人称她也叫"君夫人"。

【英　译】

The reigning prince of a state calls his wife "Madame", but she calls herself "little kid". The people of the state call her "Lady of the prince", and they call her "Our humble princess" when speaking to people of other states. The people of other states also call her "Lady of the prince".

阳货篇第十七

17.1

【原　文】

阳货欲见孔子，孔子不见，归孔子豚。孔子时其亡也，而往拜之，遇诸涂。谓孔子曰："来！予与尔言。"曰："怀其宝而迷其邦，可谓仁乎？"曰："不可。""好从事而亟失时，可谓知乎？"曰："不可。""日月逝矣，岁不我与。"

孔子曰："诺，吾将仕矣。"

【汉　译】

阳货想见孔子，孔子就是不见他，阳货就给孔子送了个礼物——一头小猪（心想孔子回拜时定要见他的）。孔子等阳货外出的时候，才去他家拜谢，不巧两人在路上碰个正着。阳货对孔子说："来！我有话跟你讲。"接着说："自己身怀本领，却看着国家迷乱而不出仕治理，这能叫作仁吗？"他继续说："这不能算作仁。""很想出仕做官，却屡次错过机会，这能叫作聪明吗？"阳货接着说："不能。""时光一天天流逝，岁月不等人呀！"

孔子说："好吧，我准备出来做官。"

【英　译】

Yang Huo desired to visit the Master who refused to meet him. Then he sent the Master a present of pig so that the Master would normally visit him with gratitude. The Master deliberately paid his visit when Yang Huo was not at home. However, he unexpectedly met Yang Huo on the way. Yang Huo said to the Master, "Come on! I would like to talk to you." Then Yang Huo said, "You're a man of extraordinary abilities, but you live a secluded life and allow your country to go astray. Can your action be called humanity?" He said continuously, "No!" Afterwards Yang Huo said, "Yo u always want to be employed by the state, but you have repeatedly missed a lot of chances. Can your action be called wisdom?" He said, "No." Yang Huo finally said, "It is a fleeting time for everyone and the transience of human life."

Confucius then said, "All right. I'll be involved in public service."

17.2

【原　文】

子曰："性相近也，习相远也。"

【汉　译】

孔子说："人的本性是相近的，因习性不同而使他们相距甚远。"

【英　译】

The Master said, "People are close to one another in their nature, but they become widely different owing to their respective behaviors."

17.3

【原　文】

子曰："唯上知与下愚不移。"

【汉　译】

孔子说："只有上等聪明之人与下等愚笨之人是不可改变的。"

【英　译】

The Master said, "It is only men of the highest intelligence and men of the most stupidity, who cannot be changed."

17.4

【原　文】

子之武城，闻弦歌之声。夫子莞尔而笑，曰："割鸡焉用牛刀？"
子游对曰："昔者偃也闻诸夫子曰：'君子学道则爱人，小人学道则易使也。'"子曰:"二三子!偃之言是也。前言戏之耳。"

【汉　译】

孔子到武城参观,听到弹琴唱歌的声音。孔子微笑道:"杀鸡,何必要用宰牛刀呀?"子游回答说:"以前我曾听先生说过,君子学了礼乐之道,就能仁爱百姓;老百姓学了礼乐之道,就容易听使唤。"孔子说:"弟子们!子游的话说得对!我刚才说的话是和他开玩笑的。"

【英　译】

The Master came to a small town named Wu Cheng, and he heard the sound of two-stringed musical instruments and singing among the people. The Master then smiled, "To kill a chicken, what's the necessity to use a knife for butchering an ox?" Zi You answered, "I have ever heard you say that the gentlemen of a country are instructed in the Way and it makes them love their fellow people, and the common people are instructed in the Way and it makes them easily to be governed." The Master said, "My dear friends, I suppose what he said is right. What I said a moment ago is just for fun."

17.5

【原　文】

公山弗扰以费畔,召,子欲往。子路不说,曰:"末之也已,何必公山氏之之也?"子曰:"夫召我者,而岂徒哉?如有用我者,吾其为东周乎?"

【汉　译】

公山弗扰占据费邑图谋反叛,召孔子前往,孔子打算去。子路不高兴,说道:"没有地方去就算了,为什么一定要到公山弗扰那里去呢?"孔子说:"那个来召我去的,难道只是白白召我去吗?倘若有人肯用我,我或许能在鲁国建立一个东周王朝呢?"

【英 译】

Gongshan Furao, a noble in the Master's native state, he held possession of Fei County as a stronghold and was plotting to rise in rebellion and then invited the Master to see him. The Master felt inclined to go. The Master's disciple, Zi Lu said unhappily, "If you can't find anywhere to go, let it go at that. Why do you think of accepting the invitation of Gongshan Furao?" The Master said, "He has invited me to see him. As for his invitation, it cannot be for nothing. If anyone employed me, I could establish a new empire in the east of China."

17.6

【原 文】

子张问仁于孔子。孔子曰："能行五者于天下，为仁矣。""请问之。"曰："恭、宽、信、敏、惠。恭则不侮，宽则得众，信则人任焉，敏则有功，惠则足以使人。"

【汉 译】

子张问孔子何为仁。孔子说："能在天下行五种美德，可称为仁。"子张又问："请问是哪五种。"孔子说："庄重，宽厚，诚信，勤敏，恩惠。庄重就不会被人戏侮，宽厚就能受到众人爱戴，诚信就会赢得别人信任，勤敏就容易获得成功，施恩惠就能很好地使唤人。"

【英 译】

Zi Zhang asked the Master what constituted humanity. The Master said, "If a man can carry out five things, he may be considered a man of humanity." Zi Zhang asked, "Would you tell me what they are?" The Master said, "They are earnestness, tolerance, trustworthiness, diligence, and favour. If you remain earnest, you will never meet with insults from others. If you are tolerant, you will win support of the people. If you keep trustworthy, you will be trusted by others. If you show great diligence, you will become successful in your cause. If you can do a favor to others, you will find that many people are willing to serve you."

17.7

【原　文】

　　佛肸召，子欲往。子路曰："昔者由也闻诸夫子曰：'亲于其身为不善者，君子不入也。'佛肸以中牟畔，子之往也，如之何？"子曰："然，有是言也。不曰坚乎，磨而不磷；不曰白乎，涅而不缁。吾岂匏瓜也哉？焉能系而不食？"

【汉　译】

　　佛肸来召孔子，孔子打算去。子路说："从前我听先生说过：'亲自做了坏事的人，君子是不去他那里的。'佛肸以中牟为据点谋反，您却要去他那里，这做何解释呢？"孔子说："是的，我是说过这些话。不是也说过，坚硬的东西磨也磨不薄；不是也说过，洁白的东西染也染不黑。难道我是一只葫芦吗？怎能老挂在那里，不让人来采食呢？"

【英　译】

A noble of a certain state, Bi Xi invited the Master to see him. The Master felt inclined to go. But the Master's disciple, Zi Lu said, "I've heard you say at one time that a good and wise man will not go to meet people who did bad things personally. Now Bi Xi is taking Zhong Mou as a stronghold to rise in rebellion. You still want to go there. How can you justify yourself to me?" The Master said, "Yes, I did say that. But is it also said, 'Hard things cannot be worn out after being ground, and white things cannot be blackened after being dyed.' How can I allow myself to be regarded as a gourd to be hung there and not be eaten?"

17.8

【原　文】

　　子曰："由也！女闻六言六蔽矣乎？"对曰："未也。""居！吾语女。好仁不好学，其蔽也愚；好知不好学，其蔽也荡；好信不好学，其蔽也贼；好直不好学，其蔽也绞；好勇不好学，其蔽也乱；好刚不好学，其蔽也狂。"

【汉　译】

孔子说："仲由，你听过有六种美德与六种弊病的说法吗？"子路回答说："没有听说过。"孔子说："你坐下，我告诉你。爱好仁德而不爱好学习，其弊病是易受人愚弄；爱好才智而不爱好学习，其弊病是放荡无归宿；爱好诚信而不爱好学习，其弊病是易受人伤害；喜好率直而不爱好学习，其弊病是言语尖刻伤人；喜好勇敢而不爱好学习，其弊病是容易酿成乱子；喜好刚强而不爱好学习，其弊病是易使人妄自尊大。"

【英　译】

The Master said, "You, have you ever heard about the six virtues and their six faults?" "No," Zhong You replied. The Master said, "Please be seated, and I will tell you. To love humanity instead of loving learning, it is liable for one to lead to foolishness. To love wisdom instead of loving learning, it is liable for one to lead to deviating from the right path. To love trustworthiness instead of loving learning, it is more prone to injury in one's feelings. To love frankness instead of loving learning, it is liable for one to make caustic comments. To love courage instead of loving learning, it is liable for one to lead to disturbance. To love the strength of character instead of loving learning, it is liable for one to be self-important."

17.9

【原　文】

子曰："小子何莫学夫《诗》？诗，可以兴，可以观，可以群，可以怨。迩之事父，远之事君；多识于鸟兽草木之名。"

【汉　译】

孔子说："弟子们，为什么不学习《诗》呢？学《诗》可以激发志气、催人奋进，可以观察世间万物及风俗民情，可以使人合群，与人和谐相处，可以抒发心中愤懑，讥讽时弊。近处讲，可以使你懂得怎样侍奉父母；远处讲，可以使你懂得如何侍奉君主；小处讲，也可使你多认识一些鸟兽草木的名称。"

【英 译】

The Master said, "My young students, why don't you study *The Book of Odes*? The Book of Odes may arouse your aspirations. It can stimulate your observation. It enables you to get on well with others and to express the resentment against injustice. From the near sight, it will enable you to support your parents with filial respect; and from the far sight, it will enable you to serve the load deferentially. Moreover, it will make you acquainted with the names of some birds, animals, plants and trees."

17.10

【原 文】

子谓伯鱼曰："女为《周南》《召南》矣乎？人而不为《周南》《召南》，其犹正墙面而立也与？"

【汉 译】

孔子对儿子伯鱼说："你学过《周南》《召南》诗吗？人若不读《周南》《召南》，就像面向墙壁而立，什么也看不到。"

【英 译】

The Master once said to his son Bo Yu, "Have you ever read the opening sections *Zhou Nan* and *Shao Nan* in *The Book of Odes*? A man who hasn't learnt Zhou Nan and Shao Nan is unable to see anything as if standing towards a wall?"

17.11

【原 文】

子曰："礼云礼云，玉帛云乎哉？乐云乐云，钟鼓云乎哉？"

【汉 译】

孔子说："礼呀礼呀，难道说只是玉帛吗？乐呀乐呀，难道仅仅是指钟鼓等乐器吗？"

【英 译】

The Master said, "The proprieties! The proprieties! Do they merely mean the presents of jades and silks? Music! Music! Does it merely mean the musical instruments of bells and drums?"

17.12

【原 文】

子曰："色厉而内荏，譬诸小人，其犹穿窬之盗也与？"

【汉 译】

孔子说："外表刚强而内心怯懦的人，如果用坏人做比喻，大概像个挖洞翻墙的小偷而已！"

【英 译】

The Master said, "A man is stern in his look but a real coward at heart. If compared to a small man, he is like a burglar who commits theft by digging a hole in the wall."

17.13

【原 文】

子曰："乡原，德之贼也。"

【汉 译】

孔子说："一乡之中全不得罪人的好好先生，是败坏道德的小人。"

【英 译】

The Master said, "A man tries not to offend anyone at the expense of principle in the village. As a matter of fact, his action is the ruin of virtue."

17.14

【原　文】

子曰："道听而涂说，德之弃也。"

【汉　译】

孔子说："在路上听到传言就四处传播，这其实是背弃了道德。"

【英　译】

The Master said, "It is actually considered as renouncing moral principles for one to preach what he has picked up on the way."

17.15

【原　文】

子曰："鄙夫可与事君也与哉？其未得之也，患得之；既得之，患失之。苟患失之，无所不至矣。"

【汉　译】

孔子说："难道可以和鄙陋之人一起侍奉君主吗？他没得到官职时，总怕得不到；已经得到了，又害怕失去。若怕失去官位，他会无所不为，什么事都干得出来。"

【英　译】

The Master said, "How is it possible to serve the lord in company with a shallow and despicable man？ Before he gains his official post, he worries lest he could not get it; after he has obtained it, he worries lest he might lose it. If he is worried about losing his position, there is nothing he can not do."

17.16

【原　文】

子曰："古者民有三疾，今也或是之亡也。古之狂也肆，今之狂也荡；古之矜也廉，今之矜也忿戾；古之愚也直，今之愚也诈而已矣。"

【汉　译】

孔子说："古代人有三种毛病，现在或许连这些毛病也没有了。古代的狂者直言无讳，现在的狂者放荡不羁；古代矜持的人威不可犯，现在矜持的人蛮横无理；古代愚蠢的人说话率直，现在愚笨的人假装直率。"

【英　译】

The Master said, "In the ancient times, men had three sorts of weaknesses, which are not to be found today. The ancient wild people were straightforward and spoke bluntly, but the present wild people are unrestrained in their actions. The ancient self-important people intended to be treated with respect, but the present self-important people appear to be rude and unreasonable. The ancient foolish people spoke without reservation, but the present foolish people pretend to be frank about their words."

17.17

【原　文】

子曰："巧言令色，鲜矣仁。"
此章与 1.3 章重复。

17.18

【原　文】

子曰："恶紫之夺朱也，恶郑声之乱雅乐也，恶利口之覆邦家者。"

【汉　译】

孔子说："我厌恶用紫色取代大红色，我厌恶郑国乐曲扰乱了典雅的正统音乐，我厌恶能说会道倾覆国家的人。"

【英　译】

The Master said, "I hate purple for displacing scarlet. I hate pop music for disturbing classical music. Finally, I hate men having the gift of gab who are liable to subvert a government."

17.19

【原　文】

子曰："予欲无言。"子贡曰："子如不言，则小子何述焉？"子曰："天何言哉？四时行焉，百物生焉，天何言哉？"

【汉　译】

孔子说："我不想再说话了。"子贡说："您如果不说话，那我们当学生的往下传述什么呢？"孔子说："天说了些什么呢？春夏秋冬四季照样运行，万物照样生长，天说了些什么呢？"

【英　译】

The Master once said, "I'd rather not say anything at all." Zi Gong said, "If you didn't want to say anymore, what would we disciples learn from you and teach to others?" The Master said, "What has the Heaven ever said? Actually, the Heaven says nothing. Yet the four seasons still move round regularly and all things in nature grow up as usual. Look at the Heaven there, and what has the Heaven ever said?"

17.20

【原　文】

孺悲欲见孔子，孔子辞以疾。将命者出户，取瑟而歌，使之闻之。

【汉 译】

孺悲想拜见孔子，孔子以生病为由推辞不见。传话的人刚走出屋门，孔子便取下瑟来边弹边唱，故意让孺悲听见。

【英 译】

A man named Ru Bei wanted to see the Master. Yet the Master declined to see him on the pretext of sickness. After the servant with the message stepping out of the door, the Master took his musical instrument Se and sang aloud deliberately to let the visitor hear it.

17.21

【原 文】

宰我问："三年之丧，期已久矣。君子三年不为礼，礼必坏；三年不为乐，乐必崩。旧谷既没，新谷既升，钻燧改火，期可已矣。"子曰："食夫稻，衣夫锦，于女安乎？"曰："安。""女安，则为之。夫君子之居丧，食旨不甘，闻乐不乐，居处不安，故不为也。今女安，则为之！"宰我出。子曰："予之不仁也！子生三年，然后免于父母之怀。夫三年之丧，天下之通丧也。予也有三年之爱于其父母乎？"

【汉 译】

宰我问："三年之丧，时间也太久了。君子三年不习礼仪，礼仪就会败坏；三年不演奏音乐，音乐也一定会失传。陈谷已吃完，新谷子已收，钻燧取火的木头也轮过一遍了，丧期一年也就够了。"孔子说："你亲丧不满三年，就吃白米饭，穿锦缎衣，你心安吗？"宰我说："心安。"孔子说："你既然觉得心安，就那样去做吧！君子守孝期间，吃美食不觉得香甜，听音乐不觉得快乐，住在家里也不觉得安适，所以才不那样做。现在你若觉得心安，你就那样去做吧！"宰我退出后，孔子说："宰我真是不仁啊！小孩子生下来，三年后才能离开父母的怀抱。守孝三年，是天下通行的丧礼，宰我难道没有得到他父母三年的怜爱吗？"

【英 译】

A disciple Zai Wo said, "I suppose that the period of three years' mourning for parents is too long. If a gentleman stops practicing the rituals for three years, the rituals are bound to be ruined; if he stops playing the music for three years, the music is bound to collapse. After all, in one year the old grains are used up and the new grains are reaped on a farm. All the four kinds of wood, through which we burn fire, have been used one after another in the four seasons of a year. Therefore, I believe that one year is enough for mourning for parents." The Master said, "You begin to eat rice and wear silks after one year's mourning. Would you feel at ease? " Zai Wo said, "Yes, I should." The Master said, "If you feel quite at ease, do it like that. During the period of three years' mourning for his parents, a very good man does not enjoy delicious food when he takes it; he does not get any pleasure when he hears music; he does not feel at ease when he lives at home. Now, since you feel at ease, do it like that." After Zai Wo having left, the Master remarked, "What a man lacking humanity he is! After he was born, a little child is unable to leave the arms of his parents until he is three years old. It is universally observed throughout the Empire regarding the period of three years' mourning for parents. After his birth, Has Zai Wo not enjoyed the affection of his parents for three years?"

17.22

【原 文】

子曰："饱食终日，无所用心，难矣哉！不有博弈者乎？为之，犹贤乎已。"

【汉 译】

孔子说："整天吃饱了饭，什么事也不想干，这种人其实很难受呀！不是有玩六博和下围棋的游戏吗？玩这个，也比没事干强。"

【英 译】

The Master said, "It's very sad for a man who is well fed all day without putting his mind to anything. Are there not such games of gambling and playing chess? Playing one of the games is even better than doing nothing at all."

17.23

【原 文】

子路曰："君子尚勇乎？"子曰："君子义以为上。君子有勇而无义为乱，小人有勇而无义为盗。"

【汉 译】

子路说："君子崇尚勇敢吗？"孔子说："君子崇尚义。君子有勇而无义，就会犯上作乱；小人有勇而无义，就会成为强盗。"

【英 译】

Zi Lu asked, "Should a good and wise man uphold bravery?" The Master said, "A good and wise man should uphold justice. A good and wise man who upholds bravery without justice is liable to offend his superiors and make trouble. A small man who upholds bravery without justice is liable to become a robber."

17.24

【原 文】

子贡曰："君子亦有恶乎？"子曰："有恶。恶称人之恶者，恶居下流而讪上者，恶勇而无礼者，恶果敢而窒者。"曰："赐也亦有恶乎？""恶徼以为知者，恶不孙以为勇者，恶讦以为直者。"

【汉 译】

子贡说："君子对人也有厌恶吗？"孔子说："有厌恶。君子厌恶宣扬别人坏处的人，厌恶处下位而毁谤上位的人，厌恶勇武而不讲礼仪的人，厌恶果敢而不通事理的人。"孔子又问："赐呀，你对人也有讨厌吗？"子贡答道："我厌恶靠抄袭别人耍聪明的人，厌恶把不谦逊视为勇敢的人，厌恶把揭发别人的隐私视为直率的人。"

【英　译】

Zi Gong said, "Does a good and wise man have his detestation for people?" The Master said, "Yes, of course. A good and wise man detests those who enjoy spreading the others' weak points; he detests those who are in inferior positions but maliciously slander their superiors; he detests those who show great courage but lack the spirit of the rituals; he detests those who are not sensible despite showing courage and determination." The Master said, "Ci, do you also have detestation for people?" Zi Gong said, "Yes, I do. I detest those who pretend to show great wisdom by plagiarizing others' work; I detest those who consider immodesty as courage; I detest those who regard disclosing others' privacy as straightforwardness."

17.25

【原　文】

子曰："唯女子与小人为难养也。近之则不孙，远之则怨。"

【汉　译】

孔子说："只有女子和小人是最难相处的。你若亲近他们，他们就会显得无礼；你若疏远他们，他们就会心生怨恨。"

【英　译】

The Master said, "It is very difficult to deal with women and small men. If you have an intimate connection with them, they will show insolence for you. If you keep your distance from them, they will complain to you."

17.26

【原 文】

子曰："年四十而见恶焉，其终也已。"

【汉 译】

孔子说："人活到四十岁还被人厌恶，他这一辈子也就完蛋了。"

【英 译】

The Master said, "If a man is still detested at the age of forty, his whole life will become a hopeless case."

微子篇第十八

18.1

【原　文】

微子去之，箕子为之奴，比干谏而死。孔子曰：“殷有三仁焉。”

【汉　译】

纣王实行暴政，微子离他而去，箕子被囚为奴隶，比干强谏而惨死。孔子说：“殷朝有三位仁人。”

【英　译】

Being resentful about the tyranny of the last king Chou of the Imperial Yin dynasty, Wei Zi (the king's elder brother) left him, Ji Zi (the king's uncle) was imprisoned and became a slave, and Bi Gan (the king's uncle) was put to death. The Master said, "There are three men of humanity in the Imperial Yin dynasty."

18.2

【原　文】

柳下惠为士师，三黜。人曰：“子未可以去乎？”曰：“直道而事人，焉往而不三黜？枉道而事人，何必去父母之邦？”

【汉　译】

柳下惠任鲁国典狱官，三次被免职。有人说：“您难道不可以离开这里吗？”柳下惠说：“如果我坚守原则，以直道待人，到哪里能不被罢免呢？如果我不讲原则，按邪道事人，又何必要离开自己的祖国呢？”

【英　译】

As an upright minister of justice in the state Lu, Liu Xiahui was removed from his post three times. Someone then said to him, "Is it not time for you to leave your country?" Liu Xiahui said, "If I adhere to the principles and honestly serve men, where can I find a good place without being dismissed in the same way? If I don't adhere to the principles and dishonestly serve men, what's the need for me to leave my native country?"

18.3

【原　文】

齐景公待孔子曰："若季氏，则吾不能；以季、孟之间待之。"曰："吾老矣，不能用也。"孔子行。

【汉　译】

齐景公谈及孔子的待遇时说："若要像鲁君对待季氏那样，我是做不到的；我要用介乎季氏和孟氏之间的礼遇对待他。"又说："我现在老了，不能用他了。"孔子便离开了齐国。

【英　译】

Regarding the treatment of the Master, Duke Jing of the state Qi said, "I can not accord him the exalted treatment as the Ji family accepted. I'd like to give him the treatment between the Ji family and the Meng family (Both the Ji and the Meng were the noble families in the state Lu). He said again, "I am growing old. I am afraid that he is unable to be engaged in my government." After hearing this, Confucius immediately took his departure from the state Qi.

18.4

【原　文】

齐人归女乐，季桓子受之，三日不朝，孔子行。

【汉　译】

齐国给鲁国送来一批歌姬舞女，季桓子接受了，他三天不理朝政，孔子便离开了鲁国。

【英　译】

Ji Huanzi, the prime minister of the state Lu, accepted a group of singing and dancing girls who were sent by the state Qi. He was so completely obsessed with them that he failed to attend the court in three days. After learning this, the Master immediately departed from his own state.

18.5

【原　文】

楚狂接舆歌而过孔子曰："凤兮凤兮！何德之衰？往者不可谏，来者犹可追。已而！已而！今之从政者殆而！"孔子下，欲与之言。趋而辟之，不得与之言。

【汉　译】

楚国狂人接舆唱着歌在孔子车前走过，他唱道："凤凰呀，凤凰呀！你的德行为何如此衰微？过去的就不要再说了，未来的还可追得上。算了，算了！现在从政者多危险呀！"孔子下车，想和他谈话，他却跑着避开了，孔子没能和他说上话。

【英　译】

Jie Yu, an eccentric man of the state Chu, passed by the Master and sang aloud, "O Phoenix, O Phoenix! How your virtue declined! The past is to let it go. Yet the future is to be cared for. Forget it! Forget it! How perilous those who went into politics!" After getting off his carriage, the Master wished to speak with him. However, the eccentric man hastened to avoid him so that the Master failed to speak with him.

18.6

【原　文】

长沮、桀溺耦而耕，孔子过之，使子路问津焉。长沮曰："夫执舆者为谁?" 子路曰:"为孔丘。"曰:"是鲁孔丘与?"曰:"是也。"
曰:"是知津矣。"问于桀溺。桀溺曰:"子为谁?"曰:"为仲由"。
曰:"是鲁孔丘之徒与?"对曰:"然。"曰:"滔滔者天下皆是也,而
谁以易之? 且而与其从辟人之士也, 岂若从辟世之士哉?"耰而不
辍。子路行以告。夫子怃然曰:"鸟兽不可与同群,吾非斯人之徒与
而谁与? 天下有道,丘不与易也。"

【汉 译】

　　长沮与桀溺两人一起在田间耕作,孔子路过他们那里,叫子路
去问他们渡口在何处。长沮说:"那个拉着缰绳的人是谁?"子路答
道:"是孔丘。"长沮说:"是鲁国那个孔丘吗?"子路答道:"是的。"
长沮说:"他自己应该知道渡口在哪里。"子路又去问桀溺。桀溺说:
"你是谁呀?"子路答道:"我是仲由。"桀溺说:"你是鲁国孔丘的弟
子吗?"子路答道:"是的。"桀溺说:"现在举世皆浊,如滔滔洪水,
谁又能改变它呢? 而且你与其跟从'避人之士'的孔丘,何不跟着我
们这些'避世之士'呢?"说完,便不停地耙土播种。子路回来,把事
情经过告诉了孔子。孔子颇有点怅然若失,说:"人是不可以与鸟兽
同群的,我不和天下人同群,又能和谁同群呢? 倘若天下有道,我
孔丘也就不会和你们一起来改变它了。"

【英 译】

　　Chang Ju and Jie Ni, two hermits, were plowing in the fields.
Meanwhile, the Master travelled past them and sent his intrepid disciple Zi
Lu to inquire them about the ford. Chang Ju said, "Who is the man that is
pulling on the reins in the carriage?" Zi Lu answered, "It is our Master."
Chang Ju asked again, "Then, is it not the Master of the state Lu?" Zi Lu
answered, "Yes, that's right." Chang Ju said, "Then, he should know
where the ford is." Zi Lu then asked another hermit Jie Ni. Jie Ni said,
"Who are you?" Zi Lu answered, "I am Zhong You." Jie Ni asked
again, "Are you not the disciple of the Master in the state. Lu?" Zi Lu
answered, "Yes, I am."

　　Jie Ni said again, "Like the overflowing floods, the whole world was
overwhelmed by the forces of darkness. Actually, the people are all the

same throughout the Empire. Who is able to change the backward situation in the country? Isn't it better for you to follow us who withdraw from society than to follow those who avoid meeting people?" After saying this, the man went on harrowing his field without stopping. Zi Lu came back and reported what had happened. The Master was disappointed to hear this, and then said, "One can not live together with the birds and the beasts. With whom shall I associate if I do not live together with humans? If the world is in order, there will be no need for me to change it with you."

18.7

【原　文】

　　子路从而后，遇丈人，以杖荷莜。子路问曰："子见夫子乎？"丈人曰："四体不勤，五谷不分，孰为夫子？"植其杖而芸。子路拱而立。止子路宿，杀鸡为黍而食之，见其二子焉。明日，子路行，以告。子曰："隐者也。"使子路反见之。至，则行矣。子路曰："不仕无义。长幼之节，不可废也；君臣之义，如之何其废之？欲洁其身，而乱大伦。君子之仕也，行其义也。道之不行，已知之矣。"

【汉　译】

　　子路跟着孔子出行，落在了后面，遇见一位老人，用拐杖挑着除草的竹器。子路问道："您看见我老师了吗？"老人说："你们这些人，四体不勤，五谷不分，谁是你的老师呢？"老人说完，把拐杖插在地上，继续除草。子路拱手站在一旁，显得很恭敬。于是老人便留子路在他家过夜，杀鸡做饭款待他，还让他的两个儿子来和子路见面。

　　第二天，子路赶上了孔子，把昨天发生的事告诉了他。孔子说："这是位隐士呀！"就让子路返回去见。等子路赶到了，老人已经出门了。子路说："人不出来做官，是不合乎道义的。长幼之间的礼节不可废弃，君臣之间的大义又怎么能废弃呢？人欲洁身自好，不出来做官，不就乱了君臣之大伦。君子出来做官，是为了推行道义。至于这些主张行不通，也早在我们预料之中。"

【英 译】

On one occasion, the Master went on a sightseeing tour and his disciple Zi Lu fell behind. Unexpectedly, Zi Lu met an old man who carried a weeding tool over his shoulder with his cane. Zi Lu asked, "Have you ever met my master?" The old man said, "You people haven't toiled with your limbs, and you can not tell the difference between the five sorts of grains. Who is your master?" After saying that, the old man planted his cane in the ground and continued weeding. Zi Lu respectfully stood along the road, by cupping one hand in the other before his chest. Deeply moved, the old man put up Zi Lu in his house for the night, killing a chicken and providing some millet pudding for him to eat. In addition, the old man presented his two sons to Zi Lu. The next day, Zi Lu caught up with the Master and reported his adventure to him. The Master said, "He is a hermit." Then he sent Zi Lu to see him again. When Zi Lu arrived, the old man was out. Zi Lu commented, "It is not reasonable for one to refuse to enter the public service. Obviously, it is unacceptable to ignore the moral responsibilities existing in the relationship between the old members and the younger ones of a family. Is it acceptable to ignore the duties a man owes to his sovereign? It's no good for one to preserve his purity and finally violate the relationship between monarch and subject. As a matter of fact, a good and wise man enters the public service to do his duty for the country. We are well aware of that, considering the principles are not accepted in the society.

18.8

【原 文】

逸民：伯夷、叔齐、虞仲、夷逸、朱张、柳下惠、少连。子曰："不降其志，不辱其身，伯夷、叔齐与！"谓："柳下惠、少连，降志辱身矣，言中伦，行中虑，其斯而已矣。"谓："虞仲、夷逸，隐居放言，身中清，废中权。""我则异于是，无可无不可。"

【汉 译】

　　隐逸之贤人有伯夷、叔齐、虞仲、夷逸、朱张、柳下惠、少连。孔子说："决不改变自己的意志，也不辱没自己的身份，这是伯夷、叔齐吧！"又说："柳下惠、少连意志改变了，身份辱没了，可他们言语能合乎伦理，行为能合乎思虑，能如此也就不错了。"又说："虞仲、夷逸，他们避世隐居，不谈政事，立身清白，弃官引退，也复合处世之道。""我则和他们不同，我怎么都行，没有什么可以的，也没有什么不可以的。"

【英 译】

There were seven men who withdrew from society, and they were Bo Yi, Shu Qi, Yu Zhong, Yi Yi, Zhu Zhang, Liu Xia Hui, and Shao Lian. The Master said, "As for Bo Yi and Shu Qi, they withdrew from the world as they would not give up their aspirations and did not want to be humiliated." The Master then said, "As for Liu Xia Hui and Shao Lian, they gave up their aspirations and they were humiliated as well. Nevertheless, what they said was found to be reasonable, and what they did was found to be considerate. It was all that they had." The Master said again, "As for Yu Zhong and Yi Yi, they led a secluded life and refused to comment on current affairs and preserved purity in their lives and resigned from their posts. They justly used their own discretion." And finally, the Master said, "As for me, I am different from such men I mentioned above. Actually, I do not care one way or the other."

18.9

【原 文】

　　大师挚适齐，亚饭干适楚，三饭缭适蔡，四饭缺适秦，鼓方叔入于河，播鼗武入于汉，少师阳、击磬襄入于海。

【汉 译】

　　太师挚去齐国了，亚饭干去楚国了，三饭缭去蔡国了，四饭缺去秦国了，打鼓的方叔到了黄河边，摇小鼓的武到了汉水旁，少师阳和击磬的襄到海滨去了。

【英　译】

At the end of Spring and Autumn　(772—481 B.C.)　in China, the famous musicians and artists of the time had to wander scattered from one state to another. Zhi, the Grand Musician, went to the state Qi; Gan, musician for the second meal, went to the state Chu; Liao, musician for the third meal, went to the state Cai; Que, musician for the forth meal, went to the state Qin; Fang Shu, the drummer reached the Yellow River; Wu, player of the rattle drum reached the River Han; Yang, the deputy of Grand Musician, and Xiang who played qing, i.e. an ancient percussion instrument made from jade or stone, reached the seashore.

18.10

【原　文】

周公谓鲁公曰："君子不施其亲，不使大臣怨乎不以。故旧无大故，则不弃也。无求备于一人！"

【汉　译】

周公对鲁公说："君子不疏远他的亲族，不使大臣抱怨自己得不到重用。老臣旧友没有重大过失，就不抛弃他们。不对个人求全责备。"

【英　译】

The Duke of Chou said to his son, the lord of the state Lu,　"A good and wise ruler should not neglect his close relations. He should not let his great ministers complain that they were not put in the important positions. He should not discard his old friends and ministers if they did not commit any serious crimes. He should not expect anybody to be perfect."

18.11

【原　文】

周有八士：伯达、伯适、仲突、仲忽、叔夜、叔夏、季随、季骃。

【汉　译】

　　周朝有八位贤士：伯达、伯适、仲突、仲忽、叔夜、叔夏、季随、季骃。

【英　译】

　　There were eight famous gentlemen in Chou Dynasty: Bo Da, Bo Kuo; Zhong Tu, Zhong Hu; Shu Ye, Shu Xia; Ji Sui and Ji Gua.

子张篇第十九

19.1

【原　文】

子张曰："士见危致命，见得思义，祭思敬，丧思哀，其可已矣。"

【汉　译】

子张说："士人在国家危难之时肯献出性命，见到所得之物能考虑是否合乎道义，祭祀时想到严肃恭敬，居丧时能想着悲伤，这样就可以了。"

【英　译】

Zi Zhang said, "A gentleman is ready to sacrifice his own life in the face of peril. He is able to think of what is right at the sight of his gain. He is able to convey his deep reverence for gods or ancestors during a sacrifice. He is able to express his sorrow in mourning. That's enough for a gentleman."

19.2

【原　文】

子张曰："执德不弘，信道不笃，焉能为有？焉能为亡？"

【汉　译】

子张说："坚守道德不弘扬，信仰道义不忠实，这样的人，怎能说他有？又怎能说他没有？"

【英　译】

Zi Zhang said, "A man adheres to the standards of virtue, but he does not develop it. He does not sincerely believe in morality and justice as well. Such a man is of little importance."

19.3

【原　文】

子夏之门人问交于子张。子张曰："子夏云何？"对曰："子夏曰：'可者与之，其不可者拒之。'"子张曰："异乎吾所闻：君子尊贤而容众，嘉善而矜不能。我之大贤与，于人何所不容？我之不贤与，人将拒我，如之何其拒人也？"

【汉　译】

子夏的学生向子张询问交友之道。子张说："你们先生子夏说了些什么？"学生答道："子夏说：'可以交友的就和他交往，不可以交友的就拒绝和他交往。'"子张说："我听到的和这不一样：君子尊敬贤人，也能容纳普通人；赞美善人，也能同情能力不足的人。倘若我是个大贤人，那对人有什么不能包容呢？倘若我不是个贤人，别人将会拒绝我，我怎么可能去拒绝别人呢？"

【英　译】

On one occasion, Zi Xia's disciples asked Zi Zhang how to make friends with others. Zi Zhang said, "What did Zi Xia say on this subject?" The disciples of Zi Xia replied, "Zi Xia said, 'Make friends with those you find good, but turn your back on those you find not good.'" Zi Zhang said, "That's different from what I've learnt. A good and wise man not only respects worthy men but also tolerates common men; he not only highly regards the good but also sympathizes with those lacking abilities. If I am a great worthy man, is there anyone I cannot tolerate? Otherwise, if I am not a worthy man, others will be able to turn their backs on me. How can I turn my back on them?"

19.4

【原　文】

　　子夏曰：“虽小道，必有可观者焉，致远恐泥，是以君子不为也。”

【汉　译】

　　子夏说：“虽是小小的技艺，也必有可观之处，但要靠它实现远大目标，恐怕是行不通的。所以君子不为小道。”

【英　译】

　　Zi Xia said, "In regard to any small skill, there is still something worthy of consideration, yet it is impossible for you to achieve great aspirations by means of it. Therefore, a wise man is not engaged in a small skill."

19.5

【原　文】

　　子夏曰：“日知其所亡，月无忘其所能，可谓好学也已矣。”

【汉　译】

　　子夏说：“每天能学到一些未知的知识，每月不忘记已学会的东西，可以说是好学的了。”

【英　译】

　　Zi Xia said, "Every day a man is able to learn what he lacks, and every month he never forgets what he has learned. Such a man is called to be eager to learn."

19.6

【原　文】

　　子夏曰：“博学而笃志，切问而近思，仁在其中矣。”

【汉 译】

子夏说："广泛地学习且能坚守其志向，恳切地提出疑问，又能紧扣主题去思考，仁道就在这中间了。"

【英 译】

Zi Xia said, "Learn extensively and remain steadfast in your aim, earnestly raise a question and ponder over it from the thematic perspective. If you study in that way, you will attain a moral life."

19.7

【原 文】

子夏曰："百工居肆以成其事，君子学以致其道。"

【汉 译】

子夏说："匠人们在作坊里完成自己的工作，读书人终身学习以实现他们的理想。"

【英 译】

Zi Xia said, "As craftsmen make their own things in the workshops so as to master their trades, so scholars dedicate themselves to learning in order to realize their ideals."

19.8

【原 文】

子夏曰："小人之过也必文。"

【汉 译】

子夏说："小人有了过失，一定会文过饰非。"

【英 译】

Zi Xia said, "When he makes a fault, a small man is sure to gloss over it."

19.9

【原　文】

子夏曰："君子有三变：望之俨然，即之也温，听其言也厉。"

【汉　译】

子夏曰："君子会有三种变化：远远望去，他很有威严；接近他后，觉得温和可亲；听他说话，感到严厉不苟。"

【英　译】

Zi Xia said, "A good and wise man gives you three different kinds of impressions. When you look at him from a distance, he appears majestic; when you come near to him, he appears gracious; when you listen to his speech, he appears severe."

19.10

【原　文】

子夏曰："君子信而后劳其民，未信则以为厉己也；信而后谏，未信则以为谤己也。"

【汉　译】

子夏说："君子要得到百姓信任后才可以使唤他们，否则百姓会认为是虐待他们；君子要得到君王信任后才可以进谏，否则君王会以为是在诽谤他。"

【英　译】

Zi Xia said, "A good and wise man who has the power should first earn the trust of common people before he works them hard, or else the common people would regard themselves being ill-treated. A good and wise man who is a public servant should first earn the trust of his lord before he ventures to point out his faults and urge him to correct them, or else the lord would regard himself being slandered."

19.11

【原　文】

　　子夏曰：“大德不逾闲，小德出入可也。”

【汉　译】

　　子夏说：“人在大节上不能逾越界限，小节上有些出入是可以的。”

【英　译】

　　Zi Xia said, "A man can not transcend moral integrity, but he may be allowed to use his discretion in the respect of trivial matters."

19.12

【原　文】

　　子游曰：“子夏之门人小子，当洒扫应对进退，则可矣，抑末也。本之则无，如之何？”子夏闻之，曰：“噫！言游过矣！君子之道，孰先传焉，孰后倦焉？譬诸草木，区以别矣。君子之道，焉可诬也？有始有卒者，其惟圣人乎！”

【汉　译】

　　子游说：“子夏的学生，做些洒水扫地和接待客人的事情是可以的，可这些都是细枝末节的小事。根本的道理却没有学到，这怎么能行呢？”子夏听到后，说：“咳！子游的话错啦！君子传授学问，哪些应先传授，哪些应后教诲呢？就和草木一样，应该分类区别对待。君子传授学问，怎么可以欺骗学生呢？能够有始有终学通透的，大概只有圣人吧!”

【英　译】

　　Zi You said "As for the younger followers of Zi Xia, they are well enough in the matters of sprinkling water and sweeping the floor and dealing with people, but all these are merely trifling details. What can they do without learning the basic principles of education?" After hearing this, Zi Xia said, "Alas, Zi You is completely mistaken! In regard to learning of a good and wise man, what should be taught first? What should be taught next? As the grasses and trees are clearly distinguished, so the pupils must be classified and taught respectively according to their capabilities. As for teaching of a good and wise man, he should not deceive his pupils. Perhaps, it is only the sage who is capable of reaching the acme of learning and teaching."

19.13

【原　文】

子夏曰："仕而优则学，学而优则仕。"

【汉　译】

子夏说："当官者有余力就去学习，学习者有余力就去做官。"

【英　译】

Zi Xia said, "An official who has surplus energy should devote himself to learning. A student who has surplus energy should enter the public service."

19.14

【原　文】

子游曰："丧致乎哀而止。"

【汉　译】

子游说："丧事做到尽哀也就够了。"

【英　译】

Zi You said, "In mourning, it's enough for you to fully express your grief."

19.15

【原　文】

子游曰："吾友张也，为难能也，然而未仁。"

【汉　译】

子游说："我的朋友子张，可以说是难能可贵了，然而还没有达到仁。"

【英　译】

Zi You said, "My friend Zi Zhang is able to do things that nobody else can do, but he hasn't attained humanity yet."

19.16

【原　文】

曾子曰："堂堂乎张也，难与并为仁矣。"

【汉　译】

曾子说："子张虽仪表堂堂，可很难和他一起做到仁。"

【英　译】

Zeng Zi said, "Zi Zhang bears a dignified appearance, but it is really difficult to live up to humanity along with him."

19.17

【原　文】

曾子曰："吾闻诸夫子：人未有自致者也，必也亲丧乎！"

【汉　译】

曾子说："我听先生说过：人的情感平时不会尽情宣泄，除非遇到父母之丧吧！"

【英 译】

Zeng Zi said, "I've heard the Master say, 'Men often do not thoroughly display their sentiment until they mourn the death of their parents.'"

19.18

【原 文】

曾子曰:"吾闻诸夫子:孟庄子之孝也,其他可能也;其不改父之臣与父之政,是难能也。"

【汉 译】

曾子说:"我听先生说过:孟庄子的孝顺,其他方面好学,旁人也能做得到,而他不改变父亲留下的家臣和父亲为政的规矩,这是别人难以做到的。"

【英 译】

Zeng Zi said, "I've heard the Master say, 'As for the filial piety of a nobleman, other men could emulate Meng Zhuangzi in the aspect of what he did on the occasion of death of his parents, but it's difficult for others to emulate him in the respect of what he did in keeping the old servants of his father and observing the polices of his father.'"

19.19

【原 文】

孟氏使阳肤为士师,问于曾子。曾子曰:"上失其道,民散久矣。如得其情,则哀矜而勿喜!"

【汉 译】

孟氏任用阳肤当典狱官,阳肤去问曾子。曾子说:"上位之人不行正道,民心离散已很久了。你若获得犯罪者的实情,应当怜悯他们,切莫居功自喜!"

【英　译】

On one occasion, the Meng family appointed Yang Fu to be a chief criminal judge, and he came to Zeng Zi for some advice. Zeng Zi said, "The rulers have not done their duties, and the common people have long suffered from low morale. If you find true and enough evidence to convict the criminals, you should show compassion for them and shouldn't become complacent about your discovery."

19.20

【原　文】

子贡曰："纣之不善，不如是之甚也。是以君子恶居下流，天下之恶皆归焉。"

【汉　译】

子贡说："纣王之无道，未必像大家说的那样过分吧！所以，君子最怕处于纣那样的不利境地，使天下的恶名都推到他身上。"

【英　译】

Zi Gong said, "The lord Zhou was the last ruler of the Shang Dynasty who was a tyrant according to legend. But I think that his wickedness is not so bad as what people said. Therefore, a good and wise man hates to be in an unfavorable situation where people will give him the bad reputation of the world."

19.21

【原　文】

子贡曰："君子之过也，如日月之食焉。过也，人皆见之；更也，人皆仰之。"

【汉　译】

子贡说："君子的过失，好像日食和月食一样。他有了过错，人人都看得见；他改正了过错，人人都敬仰他。"

【英　译】

Zi Gong said, "The faults of a gentleman are like the eclipses of the sun and the moon. When he makes a fault, all people can see it. After he corrects his fault, all people will look up to him."

19.22

【原　文】

卫公孙朝问于子贡曰："仲尼焉学？"子贡曰："文武之道，未坠于地，在人。贤者识其大者，不贤者识其小者。莫不有文武之道焉。夫子焉不学？而亦何常师之有？"

【汉　译】

卫国的公孙朝问子贡说："仲尼的学问是从哪里学来的？"子贡说："文王武王之大道，并没有失传，仍留在人间。贤者懂得其中的大道理，不贤者懂得其中的小道理，他们都传有文王武王之道。我们先生哪儿不能学习？为何非得有固定的老师？"

【英　译】

Gong Sunchao of the state Wei asked Zi Gong, "From whom did Confucius learn his knowledge?" Zi Gong said, "In the ancient Chou Dynasty of China, King Wen and King Wu held the moral principles which have not all disappeared and still exist in the world. Those who are virtuous and talented understand the great principles, and even the unworthy men understand the lesser principles. Actually, there exist the moral principles of King Wen and King Wu throughout the world. As to our master, he is able to learn the knowledge wherever he goes. Why should he necessarily have a constant teacher?"

19.23

【原　文】

叔孙武叔语大夫于朝，曰："子贡贤于仲尼。"子服景伯以告子贡。子贡曰："譬之宫墙，赐之墙也及肩，窥见室家之好。夫子之墙数仞，不得其门而入，不见宗庙之美，百官之富。得其门者或寡矣。夫子之云，不亦宜乎！"

【汉 译】

叔孙武叔在朝廷上对大夫们说："子贡比孔子贤能呀。"子服景伯就把这话告诉了子贡。子贡说："就拿围墙打比方吧，我家的围墙只有肩膀那么高，人在墙外便可看到院里房屋之好。我老师的围墙有几仞高，若你不能从大门进去，就看不到里面宗庙之美，也看不见房舍之多。能找到先生大门的人或许不多吧。叔孙武叔连孔子家的门都找不到，难怪他这么说呀！"

【英 译】

An officer of the court in the Master's native state, Shusun Wushu said to the other ministers at the imperial court, "Zi Gong is superior to his Master." Afterwards, this was reported to Zi Going by Zifu Jingbo, another minister being present at the court in the meantime. Zi Gong said, "Let's take an outer wall by analogy. My wall just reaches to the shoulders. One has to look over it, and he can see the beauty of the house. But our Master's wall is hundreds of feet high. Being unable to gain admittance through the gate, one can see neither the magnificence of the holy temple nor the sumptuousness of the official buildings. Perhaps, there are mere a few men who have found the gate. Therefore, I do not wonder that Shusun Wushu said this as he did."

19.24

【原 文】

叔孙武叔毁仲尼。子贡曰："无以为也。仲尼不可毁也。他人之贤者，丘陵也，犹可逾也；仲尼，日月也，无得而逾焉。人虽欲自绝，其何伤于日月乎？多见其不知量也。"

【汉 译】

叔孙武叔诋毁仲尼。子贡说："这样做是没有用的。仲尼是不可毁谤的。别人的贤能，也不过如丘陵，还可以超越过去；仲尼好比天上的日月，别人是无法超越的。人若要自绝于日月，那对日月又有什么损害？只表明他不自量力而已。"

【英　译】

Shusun Wushu was an officer of the imperial court in the Master's native state, and he slandered the character of the Master. On hearing of this, Zi Gong said, "It's no use for him to do that. The Master can never be defamed. The worthiness of others is like the hills which you may climb over, yet that of the Master is like the sun and the moon which you can never jump over. If one wants to isolate himself from the sun and the moon, where is the harm to the sun and the moon? It just shows that he does not take the proper measure about himself."

19.25

【原　文】

陈子禽谓子贡曰："子为恭也，仲尼岂贤于子乎？"子贡曰："君子一言以为知，一言以为不知，言不可不慎也。夫子之不可及也，犹天之不可阶而升也。夫子之得邦家者，所谓立之斯立，道之斯行，绥之斯来，动之斯和。其生也荣，其死也哀，如之何其可及也？"

【汉　译】

陈子禽对子贡说："您是谦恭吧，仲尼哪能比您还贤明呢？"子贡说："君子听人一句话，便能看出他所知，听人一句话，也能看出他所不知，所以说话可要谨慎啊！我的老师高不可及，就像天不能靠搭阶梯爬上去一样。我的老师若为诸侯或卿大夫，诚如人们所言，他教百姓自立，百姓就自立；他引导百姓，百姓就跟着走；他安抚百姓，百姓就来归顺；他动员百姓，百姓就会响应。他活着，大家都很荣耀；他死后，大家都很悲哀。这样的人，我怎么能赶得上呀？"

【英 译】

On one occasion, Chen Ziqin said to Zi Gong, "You are too courteous, aren't you? How is the Master superior to you?" Zi Gong said, "According to a single word that a man utters, a wise man is able to guess what he knows or what he doesn't know. Therefore, you should be cautious about what you say. My Master is unlikely ever to be equaled, just as no one can use the ladders to climb up the sky. If the Master became the head of a state or a noble family, he would then do the following things as what people said. The Master educated the common people to get established, and they could be established; he gave guidance for the common people, and then they followed him; he placated the common people, and they would pledge allegiance to him; he mobilized the common people, and they would agreeably support him. He is honorable when he lives; he is mourned for when he died. As for such a great man, how is it possible for us to catch up with him?"

尧曰篇第二十

20.1

【原　文】

尧曰："咨！尔舜！天之历数在尔躬，允执厥中。四海困穷，天禄永终。"舜亦以命禹。曰："予小子履，敢用玄牡，敢昭告于皇皇后帝：有罪不敢赦。帝臣不蔽，简在帝心。朕躬有罪，无以万方；万方有罪，罪在朕躬。"周有大赉，善人是富。"虽有周亲，不如仁人。百姓有过，在予一人。"谨权量，审法度，修废官，四方之政行焉。兴灭国，继绝世，举逸民，天下之民归心焉。所重民食、丧、祭。宽则得众，信则民任焉，敏则有功，公则说。

【汉　译】

尧说："唉！舜啊！按照天意，帝位传给你，你要老实坚守中正之道。若天下百姓陷入穷困之中，上天赐给你的禄位也就永远终结了。"舜也把这番话告诉给禹。商汤说（商汤在祈祷上天时说）："我小子履，谨以黑色公牛为祭品，明白地向伟大的天帝禀告：凡有罪之人，我不敢擅自赦免。天帝的臣仆，我也不敢埋没，都按您的意愿来选择。倘若我自身有罪，不要连累天下万方；若天下万方有罪，那罪就由我一人来担当。"

周朝恩赐天下，让贤人得到富贵。（武王）说："我虽然有至亲，但不如有仁人。百姓若有过错，责任全在我一人。"

（孔子说）：谨慎审查度量衡，规范法律制度，恢复废弃的官职，天下政令便可畅通。复兴被灭亡了的国家，接续已断绝的世族后代，选用被遗落的先朝旧臣，天下百姓也就心悦诚服了。

（当政者）应重视为民办三件事：粮食、丧礼、祭礼。

（当政者）宽厚，就能得到众人拥护；讲诚信，就能赢得民众信任；勤敏行事，就能取得功绩；秉公办事，百姓就会高兴。

280

【英　译】

The Chinese ancient emperor Yao abdicated in favor of Shun, his successor. And Yao said, "Alas! Shun! The order of succession ordained by God has fallen upon you. You should wholeheartedly stick to the middle course of right. If the common people are caught in strained circumstances within the Empire, your position as a sovereign will be taken away from you forever." Afterwards the emperor Shun said the same language when in his old age he abdicated in favor of his successor Yu.

The first emperor Tang of Shang dynasty, when he offered up his prayers to God, he said, "I, Lu, dare to offer Thee a black bull as a sacrifice and to make a declaration for the sovereign Lord. I dare not pardon the sinners; I shall present Thy servants who are selected by Thee alone. If I do commit an offence, let not the common people suffer for my offence. But if the common people commit offences, let me bear the punishment of their offences."

The Chou dynasty granted favors to the people throughout the Empire, and let the good people become rich. The lord Wu of the Chou dynasty said, "I have the closest relatives, but it's better for me to have men of humanity. If the common people commit errors, let me bear the penalty of their errors."

The government should carefully examine the weights and measures, cautiously lay down the legal systems, and re-establish disused official positions. In this way, the government decrees throughout the Empire will be effectively implemented. They should also restore the annexed states, succeed the extinct descendants of clans, and select the stifled talents of previous dynasty. Thus, the common people throughout the Empire will delightedly acknowledge their sovereign.

They should pay serious attention to food for the people, funerals for the dead, and sacrificial rituals.

Being tolerant and generous, they will be able to win support of the people. Being trustworthy, they will be able to gain confidence of the people. Being quick and diligent, they will be able to achieve success. If they are impartial, the common people will become very pleased.

20.2

【原　文】

　　子张问于孔子曰："何如斯可以从政矣？"子曰："尊五美，屏四恶，斯可以从政矣。"

　　子张曰："何谓五美？"子曰："君子惠而不费，劳而不怨，欲而不贪，泰而不骄，威而不猛。"

　　子张曰："何谓惠而不费？"子曰："因民之所利而利之，斯不亦惠而不费乎？择可劳而劳之，又谁怨？欲仁而得仁，又焉贪？君子无众寡，无小大，无敢慢，斯不亦泰而不骄乎？君子正其衣冠，尊其瞻视，俨然人望而畏之，斯不亦威而不猛乎？"

　　子张曰："何谓四恶？"子曰："不教而杀谓之虐；不戒视成谓之暴；慢令致期谓之贼；犹之与人也，出纳之吝谓之有司"。

【汉　译】

　　子张向孔子问道："怎样做可以从政呢？"孔子说："尊崇五美，摒弃四恶，这样就可以从政了。"

　　子张问道："什么叫五美呢？"孔子说："君子施惠于民而自己又不破费，能役使百姓而不招致其怨恨，心有欲望而不贪婪，性情安泰而不骄傲，仪态威严而不凶猛。"

　　子张问道："什么叫给人恩惠而自己又不破费？"孔子说："让百姓做对自己有利的事，不就能使他们得到好处，而又不劳民伤财吗？选择百姓能做的事让他们去劳作，又有谁会怨恨呢？想要仁便得到了仁，还贪什么呢？君子对人，无论人多人少，不管是大是小，都不敢怠慢，这不就是性情安泰而不骄傲吗？君子衣冠整齐，目不斜视，态度庄重，使人望之而生敬畏之心，这不就是仪态威严而不凶猛吗？"

　　子张问道："什么叫四恶呢？"孔子说："弃民不教而加以杀戮，叫作虐；事先不告诫百姓，而临时责其成功，叫作暴；开始懈怠不问，却突然下令限期完成，这叫贼；同样是给人财物，出手时却不免吝啬，这叫作小家子气。"

【英 译】

Zi Zhang asked the Master, "What should be done for one to go into politics?" The Master said, "Observe the five good principles and discard the four bad principles. By doing so, he is able to go into politics."

Zi Zhang said, "What is meant by the five good principles?" The Master said, "A good and wise man does something that will benefit the common people without wasting his resources; he works them hard without causing their complaints; he has desires without being greedy; he remains composed without being arrogant; he is awe-inspiring without being fierce."

Zi Zhang said, "What is meant by 'benefitting the common people without wasting his resources'?" The Master said, "It is to encourage the people to undertake the profitable labor which will benefit them, is this not 'benefitting the common people without wasting his resources'? If a good and wise man selects what the common people are able to bear, who will have any causes for complaint? If he desires benevolence, a man is able to gain it. So, is it necessary to be greedy? Whether he deals with a few people or with many people, whether he deals with the great force of people or with the small force of people, a good and wise man is never presumptuous for them. Is this not 'remaining composed without being arrogant'? A good and wise man is always fully dressed. He is respected by looking at the people directly, and he is also awe-inspiring at the first sight. Is this not 'being awe-inspiring without being fierce'?"

Zi Zhang said, "What is meant by the four bad principles?" The Master said, "To execute the people without first educating them is called cruelty. To demand them an immediate success without giving public notice in advance is called tyranny. To demand their success with the time limit when slacking off instruction at first is called doing serious harm to people. Not to be generous when giving possessions for the people is called stinginess."

20.3

【原　文】

孔子曰："不知命，无以为君子也；不知礼，无以立也；不知言，无以知人也。"

【汉　译】

孔子说："不知天命，就不能做君子；不懂得礼，就不能自立于社会；不懂别人说的话，就不能理解他人。"

【英　译】

The Master said, "A man can not be a good and wise man if he does not know his own destiny; a man can not get established in society if he does not know the rituals; a man cannot judge the character of men if he does not know their use of language."